Immaterial **Objects**

Immaterial **Objects**

Works from the

Permanent Collection

of the

Whitney Museum of American Art

New York

Richard Marshall

**This exhibition and catalogue are sponsored by the
National Committee of the Whitney Museum of American Art,
with additional support from the National Endowment for the Arts.**

Exhibition Itinerary:

North Carolina Museum of Art, Raleigh

October 14-December 31, 1989

Albany Museum of Art, Georgia

January 12-February 25, 1990

San Jose Museum of Art, California

July 21-September 23, 1990

Curatorial assistance and research:

Peter Doroshenko, Anne Long, Susan Woods

Catalogue Design: Barbara Balch

Printing: Eastern Press

Cover Paper: Champion Carnival®; Courtesy of
Champion International Corporation

ISBN 0-87427-068-5

Contents

Foreword *Tom Armstrong*

Throughout its history, the Whitney Museum of American Art has actively supported living American artists through a vigorous program of acquisitions and exhibitions. The Museum has always considered collecting the art of its own time to be one of its primary purposes. This dedication to the work of living artists, which began with the efforts of Gertrude Vanderbilt Whitney as early as 1908 and has continued since the Museum was founded by her in 1930, has led to the formation of the most comprehensive collection of twentieth-century American art. In many instances during the past two decades, we have acquired temporal, experimental works which other museums would find difficult to assimilate into their collections and programs. This work has a particular relevance to the intellectual concerns of American artists of the period and, therefore, is important for the public to see if the character and strength of American artistic achievements during this time are to be understood.

The National Committee of the Whitney Museum of American Art, formed in 1980, sponsors projects each year to make the resources of the Whitney Museum available to a wider public. The Committee consists of forty-eight members from twenty-four states. By making this exhibition possible, they have brought new ideas and visions to a broader audience than we would otherwise serve, and we are grateful to the National Committee for its assistance in presenting this material. We hope it will stimulate people to reconsider their environment through new concepts of looking and appreciating space, light, time, and other phenomena that engage these artists. Richard Marshall, curator, the Trustees and staff of the Whitney Museum, and I join our partners, the National Committee, in helping you celebrate American art.

Introduction *Richard Marshall*

"Immaterial Objects" presents sculpture by sixteen artists who sought to redefine and dematerialize the art object. These works, made primarily in the 1960s and 1970s, reject the fixed, permanent objectness of traditional sculpture, taking it off the pedestal to occupy space in new ways. The sculpture presented here is not completely immaterial but possesses a physicality or configuration that is often malleable, evasive, or temporal. Seen together, the works display overlapping and interrelated aspects of three prominent sculptural concerns: immateriality, installational technique, and environmental impact. Dan Flavin, Robert Irwin, and James Turrell use the immaterial phenomenon of light as the main element of their pieces; Mel Bochner, Jonathan Borofsky, and Sol LeWitt create works that exist only when assembled and installed on the floor or when drawn or painted directly onto the wall; and the configurations made by Vito Acconci, Mary Lucier, and Dennis Oppenheim are environmental in their incorporation of sound or video and experiential rather than solely visual, audio, or physical in their impact.

There exist precedents for such an approach to art-making in Marcel Duchamp's installations and motorized objects, Kurt Schwitters' architectural environments, Alexander Calder's mobiles, and Dada performance events. A more comprehensive rejection of traditional formal sculptural concerns, however, only emerged in America during the 1960s, when artists began to expand upon or break away from the weight and substance of Minimal art by introducing the elements of chance, time, and temporality as integral components. This drive to make impermanent, nonmaterialistic, and site-specific objects does not fall under the heading of a single movement or generation; rather, over the past twenty-five years, it has incorporated various aspects of Minimalism, Conceptualism, and post-Minimalism. Each artist has adapted a particular aesthetic in order to achieve alternative sculptural forms. A Minimalist approach, as exemplified by Andre, Flavin, and Turrell, focuses on pristine geometric form and purity of materials. Conceptual attitudes, as seen in the work of LeWitt and Bochner, stress pure idea and system over physical realization. A post-Minimal emphasis on infusing abstract objects with content and illusion is found in the sculptures of Nauman, Tuttle, and Saret. Though diverse in materials and concept, all these works are characterized by elements of modularity, temporality, variability, and a sometimes ephemeral nature. They reveal the attempt of contemporary artists to make objects that question the nature and limits of a three-dimensional object, allowing it to exist in an area that transcends the mere physical presence to envelop sight, sound, architecture, and experience.

The works in the exhibition cluster into four or five interrelated groupings that exhibit shared concerns and related principles of construction or installation. Among the earliest are those representing a strict Minimalist approach as employed by Flavin, Irwin, and Turrell—all of which take light as the primary medium and are consequently the most immaterial of the pieces in the exhibition. Flavin's *Untitled (for Robert, with fond regards)* (1977) is constructed of twelve industrially manufactured fluorescent tubes and fixtures arranged in a grid configuration that spans a corner. Three horizontal pink tubes and three yellow tubes face the viewer, and six vertical red tubes face the corner. The mixtures of these colored lights and the way they activate and interact with the existing architecture of the room are what constitute the artwork. The immaterial phenomenon of light creates the art and supersedes the physical construction of the gridded metal and glass tubes. In a related manner, James Turrell's *Shanta* (1967) presents a seemingly solid geometric form floating in the corner of an empty room. However, the illusion is created by bright, white xenon light projected from a fixture attached to the ceiling onto the surface of the wall. Turrell's desire to challenge perceptual awareness and to give light a solidity and physicality is enhanced by his specifications that the room be dark, quiet, and empty.

Robert Irwin's untitled disk piece of 1966–67 also incorporates artificial light but with a more subtle and subliminal effect. Like Turrell, Irwin is interested in perceptual phenomena and is attempting to make the physical object dematerialize, leaving only the impression of light, shape, and color. To achieve this, he designed a circular convex disk that projects away from the wall, seeming to float in space. The disk is then cross-lit by four lights—two from above and two from below—that create four distinct, circular shadows on the wall, noticeably darker in the four areas where the shadows overlap. As a result, the disk, the shadows, and the surrounding wall all become one, creating an environmental experience. After staring at the center of the disk for a few minutes, the edges begin to vanish and the physicality of the object evaporates, so that the shadows become more materialistic and prominent and confuse issues of form, substance, and reality.

Carl Andre utilizes a strict reductivist approach to sculpture with a modular repetition of twenty-nine equal squares of commercially fabricated and cut copper. While emphasizing the physicality and mass of the materials, he conversely makes the object immaterial by having it exist on the same plane as the floor, even allowing it to be walked on. This process negates the volumetric displacement of space that is essential to a traditional sculptural presence. Like most of the objects here, this work only takes final form when it is installed—laid out in a single line with one edge grounded against a wall, thus attached to and responding to the architecture. Andre reinforces the elemental nature of the piece by using a pure, or cardinal, number of plates that is only divisible by one and titling it accordingly—*Twenty-Ninth Copper Cardinal* (1975).

Richard Serra's imposing *Left Corner Rectangles* (1979), like the works of Flavin, Turrell, Irwin, and Andre, relies on the architectural setting for its realization. It consists of two vertical rectangles of linen that have been densely covered with black oil paintstick and stapled directly to the wall, meeting at the corner. Although existing on the same plane as the walls, Serra's piece perceptually creates a third dimension of dense atmosphere—a cubic space in the corner defined by the weighty, yet two-dimensional rectangles.

Mel Bochner, Sol LeWitt, and Jonathan Borofsky approach the problem of creating an immaterial object from a conceptual vantage point. All three give primary importance to the original idea rather than its physical execution. Each work exists initially as a written set of instructions, diagrams, or sketches. The actual art object is not realized until the instructions for its creation are executed by the artist—or by others. The artist has authored the work, but does not necessarily have to make it. He has removed himself from the act of making by stating the idea for the art. Mel Bochner's *Ten to 10* (1972) comprises 110 white stones laid out on the floor in a fixed arrangement prescribed by the artist and diagrammed in detailed instructions for installation. The stones are configured into two concentric circles; the stones in the inner circle decrease by one stone at each location as it moves clockwise, while the outer circle increases by one stone at each location until it culminates in the numeral 10, made up of ten stones. The work visualizes the conceptual process of counting and illustrates the formation of marks as a symbol for a numeral in the form of a three-dimensional sculpture.

In a similar way, LeWitt's *Lines to Points on a Six Inch Grid* (1976) is the visual realization of a set of directions specifying the number of lines that emanate from given points on a wall. In its entirety, the work is an enclosed, four-sided, black room, each wall becoming more complex and dense with an increasing number of white lines. LeWitt has further distanced himself from the execution of the work by allowing the size and texture of the walls to be determined by different architectural circumstances and by allowing the draftsman executing the work to decide the end point of each line, so long as it terminates at an intersection on the underlying six-inch pencil grid. Borofsky's *Running People at 2,616,216* (1979) also allows for variations of size and configuration in the final execution. Borofsky selected a small, scribbled image of figures in motion from one of his own drawings and converted it into a transparency that can be projected onto the wall, traced, and painted in black latex. Like LeWitt, Borofsky wants to use the existing architecture to make the work environmental and assertive, allowing the image to traverse corners, doorways, moldings, and ceilings. Again, the work only exists when it is executed, and it is painted over after any given exhibition period. By incorporating three-dimensional architectural features, Borofsky achieves a sculptural presence from an immaterial, two-dimensional image. And like Bochner, he also integrates the conceptual aspect of counting by assigning the work a number that reflects its particular location in his ongoing sequence of enumeration. In this way, he symbolically joins two distinct, yet related, aspects of his aesthetic—the linear and conceptual with the emotional and representational.

The work of Bruce Nauman, Alan Saret, and Richard Tuttle displays a shift away from purely minimal and conceptual modes that eliminate any associative content. Their pieces are infused with implied references or allusions to something outside the form itself or to the specific materials of its making. Nauman's *Untitled* (1965–66) is made up of a number of latex-soaked strips of burlap that are connected at one end. The strips remain soft and flexible and take on a different arrangement each time they are bunched on the floor. While the properties of the material predetermine the range of configurations, the work's possible forms or meanings are not fixed or rigid. Alan Saret's *True Jungle: Canopy Forest* (1968) also allows the physical properties of the material to determine its sculptural form. Saret has chosen to use an open, gridded wire that is more air than matter. The piece is composed of modules of painted, galvanized wire attached to nails in the wall, allowing an arched, three-dimensional form. Each time the work is installed, the wire sections are randomly placed so that the resulting configuration differs for each installation. But the work's reliance on chance, process, and material is overshadowed by the visual allusion—strengthened by the descriptive title—to a type of forest of horizontal strata (or "canopies") that supports a subsystem of animal or vegetable life.

Tuttle's *Grey Extended Seven* (1967), like the Nauman and Saret pieces, uses a barely altered material that displays the properties of its making. Tuttle's desire to make quiet, unobtrusive objects is achieved here by cutting an eccentric octagonal form in canvas, dyeing it a washy gray-tan color, and hanging it unstretched on the wall with pins. The piece is both sculptural and painterly, rigid and loose, hard and soft, there and not there. Tuttle further confounds our perceptual expectations by sometimes exhibiting these works on the floor, which confuses their identity as objects and permits various interpretations.

The work of both George Sugarman and Judy Pfaff is strongly materialistic in its physical makeup. But, in an analogous way to the other artists discussed, Sugarman and Pfaff attempt to lessen the mass of the object by structuring the sculpture with disparate, unconnected forms in an open, airy configuration. Both diverge from the reductive, minimal expression that characterizes many of the works presented here by being much more inclusive and expansive and by introducing energetic forms and bright colors. Sugarman's *Inscape* (1964) suggests an internalized landscape in a chaotic yet calculated arrangement of painted wood forms on the floor. The eccentrically shaped pieces seem to be randomly strewn about, but, in fact, they are specifically placed in accordance with the artist's directions in an open oval arrangement that allows for internal relationships between forms and colors. Like Andre's floor-based sculpture and Saret's multiple-component object, Sugarman's work offers a novel solution to the problem of making an object that is both flexible and modular and simultaneously volumetric and spatial.

Pfaff's *Supermercado* (1986) achieves a similar goal in a more frenetic explosion of shapes and colors. Made up of a number of elements attached to the wall in an expansive arrangement, it dematerializes the overall mass of the objects. Pfaff's choice of materials, like the supermarket referred to in the title, is a conglomeration of commercially made things—bowls, wire forms, wood grids, spheres, decorative grille work—which gives a popular, consumerist reference to the work. The seemingly random placement of the numerous elements in the sculpture is misleading because, as in Sugarman's sculpture, there is a prescribed order for the parts. This type of predetermined order is atypical for Pfaff, however, whose usual practice is to create a completely random, room-size environment that requires the viewer to move through space in order to experience it.

The works by Dennis Oppenheim, Vito Acconci, and Mary Lucier offer another aspect of immaterial object-making. Their pieces are completely environmental and participatory; the viewer must experience the sculpture rather than look at it. Oppenheim's *Lecture #1* (1976–83) consists of a room filled with small wooden chairs facing a lectern at which stands a small dummy with a moving jaw. The dummy's mouth is synchronized with a taped lecture of fictitious art historical facts outlining how "American artists whom had surfaced during the sixties were the target of a carefully planned series of assassinations beginning in 1973 with the death of Robert Smithson." The marionette is a surrogate self-portrait, standing in for Oppenheim so that he can escape any attempts on his own life. The entire tableau incorporates many of the features previously discussed—modular components, temporal existence of an installation, room-size flexible dimensions, and environmental exigencies. To these, Oppenheim has added the dimension of sound and specific, although invented, subject matter and content.

Acconci's *False Center for L.A. (or The New York Address)* (1978–79) also includes a tape-recorded sound track in an environmental piece that invites, yet thwarts, viewer participation. Four severely geometric chairs with tall backs face each other, forming a tight square that does not allow entry or seating. The back of each chair contains a speaker; each one alternately emits the same monotonous repetition of phrases and sounds, as if engaged in an imaginary monologue. This forces the viewer into a voyeuristic involvement with the work, trying to decipher its message and meaning. Acconci has devised an eerie space that incorporates light, sound, and object and culminates in a sculptural experience greater than its individual parts. Lucier has created a more elaborate environment in *Ohio at Giverny* (1983). A room-size installation of video monitors with a sound track, the piece is a romantic exploration of light in the landscape of the two locations noted in the title. In a similar way to Oppenheim and Acconci, Lucier deals with specific locales and subject matter in an installational and environmental manner, but the actual substance of the artwork transcends the physical attributes of the piece to become an experiential involvement in space, time, light, color, and movement.

Collectively, these artists have forged new precepts of sculpture making. Seeking to reject the traditional methods of carving, casting, and modeling, they have introduced a new vocabulary of materials, methods, and situations. They have developed art forms that do not have to be made in the studio and do not have to be made by the artist. They have shifted sculpture's traditional configuration from vertical to horizontal and allowed it to incorporate language, light, architecture, and sound. These artists have redefined the parameters of art and demonstrated that a sculpture can be immaterial and still be an object.

Vito **Acconci**

Over the period of the last twelve years certain of my works have traced a method of dealing with activities in space....Space is something that passes in front of you or beside you, the kind of space that you see while looking out a car window, looking out a train window, walking down a street....Place is a kind of battlefield—the notion that taking a place means taking it away from someone else. Space as domain, space as boundary, space as a kind of power....Space can be the mapping of space—topological diagrams, perspective drawings. A space can be controlled by taking it in hand and putting it down on paper....The map of a space can become nationalized: a space with a flag, space as a kind of specific historical/political cultural space, designed for a particular community of viewers....The notion of urban space, or particularly New York space, as a tangible rather than a visible space. New York is a city that you hear and touch, a city that you feel your way around in....Recent works have dealt with space as enclosure, often as models without actual accommodation for activities. I'm beginning now to tie pieces into existing architecture, using a specific place as an aspect of work instead of isolating my work from the larger environment.

Vito Acconci, "Site: The Meaning of Place in Art and Architecture," *Design Quarterly*, no. 122 (Summer 1983), p. 4.

False Center for L.A. (or The New York Address), 1978–79
Painted wood construction, speakers, amplifier, quadrophonic tape deck, and
mushroom lamp, 96 1/2 x 49 3/4 x 49 3/4 inches
Whitney Museum of American Art, New York; Purchase, with funds from the
Gilman Paper Company and the National Endowment for the Arts   79.32

Installation **Instructions**

A piece by a New York artist intended for a space—and an audience.

The space is a conventional gallery room, about forty feet by twenty-five feet. The room is dark. At the entrance, facing viewers as they enter, is a sculpture stand about four feet high: a small spotlight marks the title, white letters on a black ground. Away from the entrance, off in a corner, a larger spotlight marks the piece: four white chairs facing each other, placed edge to edge—the chairs make a hollow square in the middle of themselves (to sit down a viewer has to climb up and over, up and in).

Behind each chair is a white sculpture stand holding an audio speaker. The sound goes from speaker to speaker, around in a circle: the sound is a 'round,' a song. As the song goes from here to there (speaker to speaker), it goes from here to there (New York to Los Angeles, Los Angeles to New York).

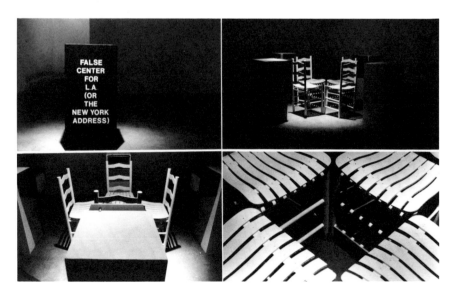

False Center for L.A. (or The New York Address)
as originally installed at the Los Angeles Institute of Contemporary Art, 1976.

It seems to me now that, although the piece was originally designed for a space in Los Angeles (the 'goal' of the piece), it can just as easily be set up in New York (the 'origin' of the piece). In fact, it can probably be set up anywhere in the United States; once the two points (NY and LA) have been set up, wherever the piece is can function as a pointer to those points.

It seems to me also that the installation can be improved. Originally the installation consisted of ready-made chairs, with accompanying speakers. Better, I think, if the piece includes a construction that can function as chairs (chairs that, in turn, can contain speakers, in a construction that includes its own spotlight).

DIAGRAM FOR REVISED INSTALLATION:

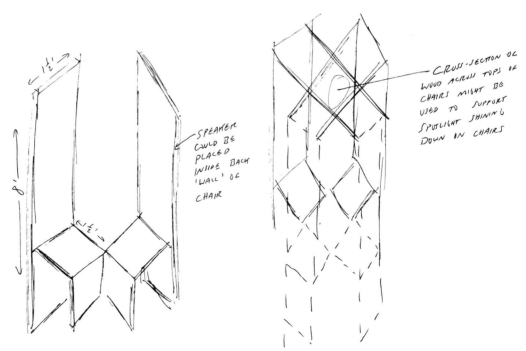

SPEAKER COULD BE PLACED INSIDE BACK 'WALL' OF CHAIR

CROSS-SECTION OF WOOD ACROSS TOPS OF CHAIRS MIGHT BE USED TO SUPPORT SPOTLIGHT SHINING DOWN IN CHAIRS

Audiotape Transcript

Speaker 1	Speaker 2	Speaker 3	Speaker 4
Ba-ba-ba-	Ba-		
	Ba-	Ba-ba-ba-ba-ba-	Ba-
Ba-ba-ba-	Ba-	Ba-ba-ba-ba-ba-	Ba-
We won't—	worry—		
We won't—	care—	And they don't—	care—
They don't—	dare—	Whatever they—	dare—
1-2-3-4		Until we—	die—
Ba-	Ba-ba-ba-	Ba-	
Ba-	Ba-ba-ba-	Ba-	Ba-ba-ba-ba-ba-
	We love—	them—	Ba-ba-ba-ba-ba-
Us—	We fear—	them—	And they hate—
Us—	We hate lov-	ing—	So they love—
Them—	1-2-3-4-	Ba-ba-ba-	That we live for—
Ba-ba-ba-ba-ba-	Ba-	Ba-ba-ba-	Ba-
Ba-ba-ba-ba-ba-	Ba-	We come—	Ba-
And they stay—	there—	We go—	here—
To bring them—	here—	They get it—	there—
And take it—	there—	1-2-3-4-	here—
		Ba-ba-ba-	

Speaker 1	Speaker 2	Speaker 3	Speaker 4
Ba-	Ba-ba-ba-ba-ba-	Ba-	
Ba-	Ba-ba-ba-ba-ba-	Ba-	Ba-ba-ba-
stop—	And they won't—	go—	We won't—
round—	To hold them—	in—	We go a—
off—	What they stop—	hold—	They keep us—
Ba-ba-ba-	Ba-	Ba-ba-ba-ba-ba-	1-2-3-4-
Ba-ba-ba-	Ba-	Ba-ba-ba-ba-ba-	Ba-
We won't grow—	old—	We'll only—	Ba-
We'll leave no—	trace—	That they can—	die—
They'll look for—	us—	In their dreams of—	find—
1-2-3-4-	Ba-ba-ba-	Ba-	them—
Ba-	Ba-ba-ba-	Ba-	Ba-ba-ba-ba-ba-
Ba-	We have no—	where—	Ba-ba-ba-ba-ba-
here—	We go from—	here—	To grow from—
are—	We are—	what—	To who we—
be—	1-2-	3-	They hate to think they could—
			4-

Born in the Bronx, New York, 1940
Studied at Holy Cross College, Worcester, Massachusetts
(B.A., 1962); University of Iowa, Iowa City (M.F.A., 1964)
Lives in Brooklyn, New York

SELECTED ONE-ARTIST EXHIBITIONS

1969   Rhode Island School of Design, Providence
1971   John Gibson Gallery, New York
1972   California Institute of the Arts, Valencia
         Sonnabend Gallery, New York
1973   Galleria Schema, Florence
         Sonnabend Gallery, New York
1975   Museum of Conceptual Art, San Francisco
         Portland Center for the Visual Arts, Oregon
1976   The Kitchen, New York
         Anthology Film Archives, New York
1977   Centre d'Art Contemporain, Geneva
         The Clocktower, Institute for Art and Urban Resources, New York
         University Gallery, University of Massachusetts, Amherst
1978   Stedelijk Museum, Amsterdam
         Whitney Museum of American Art, New York
1979   Sonnabend Gallery, New York
1980   Museum of Contemporary Art, Chicago
1981   Kölnischer Kunstverein, Cologne
         Padiglione d'Arte Contemporanea, Milan
1984   Gallery Nature Morte, New York
1985   The Brooklyn Museum, New York
         Wadsworth Atheneum, Hartford
1986   University of South Florida Art Galleries, Tampa

SELECTED GROUP EXHIBITIONS

1969   Dwan Gallery, New York, "Language III"
         Seattle Art Museum, "557,087"
1970   The Museum of Modern Art, New York, "Information"
1972   Kassel, West Germany, "Documenta 5"
1973   Whitney Museum of American Art, New York, "American Drawings 1963–1973"
1974   The Art Institute of Chicago, "71st American Exhibition"
         The Museum of Modern Art, New York, "Eight Contemporary Artists"
1976   Venice, Italy, "37th Biennale di Venezia"
1977   Institute of Contemporary Art, University of Pennsylvania, Philadelphia, "Improbable Furniture"
         Whitney Museum of American Art, New York, "1977 Biennial Exhibition"
1978   Stedelijk Museum, Amsterdam, "Made by Sculptors"
1979   P.S.1, Institute for Art and Urban Resources, New York, "Sound"
1982   Kassel, West Germany, "Documenta 7"
1984   Hirshhorn Museum and Sculpture Garden, Smithsonian Institution, Washington, D.C., "Content: A Contemporary Focus, 1974–1984"
         Hayden Gallery, Massachusetts Institute of Technology, Cambridge, "Visions of Paradise: Installations by Vito Acconci, David Ireland, and James Surls"

SELECTED BIBLIOGRAPHY

Acconci, Vito, Marja Bloem, and Dorine Mignot. *Vito Acconci* (exhibition catalogue). Amsterdam: Stedelijk Museum, 1978.

Herzogenrath, Wulf. *Vito Acconci: Arbeiten in Deutschland, 1979–1981/Workshop in Zurich* (exhibition catalogue). Cologne: Kölnischer Kunstverein; Zurich: Kunsthaus Zürich, 1981.

Kirshner, Judith Russi. *Vito Acconci: A Retrospective 1969–1980* (exhibition catalogue). Chicago: Museum of Contemporary Art, 1980.

Kunz, Martin. *Vito Acconci* (exhibition catalogue). Lucerne: Kunstmuseum Luzern, 1978.

Licht, Jennifer. *Eight Contemporary Artists* (exhibition catalogue). New York: The Museum of Modern Art, 1974.

Carl **Andre**

My sculptures are masses and their subject is matter.

Carl Andre, statement dated June 28, 1989, Artists' Files, Whitney Museum of
American Art, New York.

Twenty-Ninth Copper Cardinal, 1975

Twenty-nine copper plates, 3/16 x 20 x 20 inches each,

3/16 x 20 x 580 inches overall

Whitney Museum of American Art, New York; Purchase, with funds from the

Gilman Foundation, Inc. and the National Endowment for the Arts   75.55

TITLE OF WORK: TWENTYNINTH COPPER CARDINAL

DATE OF WORK: 1975

MATERIAL: COPPER PLATE

NUMBER AND CONFIGURATION OF ELEMENTS: 29-UNIT LINE (1 X 29) EXTENDING FROM BASE OF WALL

DIMENSIONS OF EACH ELEMENT: 0.5 CM X 50 CM X 50 CM EACH

OVERALL DIMENSIONS: 0.5 CM X 50 CM X 1450 CM OVERALL

PLACE OF ORIGIN: ROME

DOCUMENTATION/AUTHENTICATION: THIS SHEET

DATE AND PLACE OF ACQUISITION: 1976 NEW YORK

SOURCE OF ACQUISITION: SPERONE-WESTWATER-FISCHER, INC

METHOD OF ACQUISITION (PURCHASE, TRADE, GIFT, OTHER): PURCHASE

PRESENT LOCATION: THE WHITNEY MUSEUM OF AMERICAN ART

EXHIBITION HISTORY: GALLERIA SPERONE, PALAZZO DEL DRAGO, ROMA, 1975; SPERONE-WESTWATER-FISCHER, INC., NEW YORK, 1975

THIS WORK
ROME
1975
@

THIS SHEET
NEW YORK
10 FEB 76
@

Twenty-Ninth Copper Cardinal, 1975

Lever, 1966

137 fire bricks, 4 1/2 x 8 7/8 x 2 1/2 inches each,

4 1/2 x 8 7/8 x 348 inches overall

National Gallery of Canada, Ottawa

Born in Quincy, Massachusetts
Studied at Phillips Academy, Andover, Massachusetts (1951–53)
Lives in New York

SELECTED ONE-ARTIST EXHIBITIONS

1965	Tibor de Nagy, New York
1967	Dwan Gallery, Los Angeles
	Galerie Konrad Fischer, Düsseldorf
1968	Galerie Heiner Friedrich, Munich
	Irving Blum Gallery, Los Angeles
	Städtisches Museum, Mönchengladbach, West Germany
1969	Dwan Gallery, New York
	Haags Gemeentemuseum, The Hague, The Netherlands
1970	The Solomon R. Guggenheim Museum, New York
1973	Institute of Contemporary Art, Boston
	The Museum of Modern Art, New York
1975	Kunsthalle Bern, Switzerland
	Sperone Westwater Fischer Gallery, New York
1978	Albright-Knox Art Gallery, Buffalo
	Whitechapel Art Gallery, London
1979	The Art Institute of Chicago
	Dallas Museum of Fine Arts
1980	Paula Cooper Gallery, New York
	National Gallery of Canada, Ottawa
1981	Museum Haus Lange, Krefeld, West Germany
	Württembergischer Kunstverein, Stuttgart
1987	Haags Gemeentemuseum, The Hague, The Netherlands
	Stedelijk Van Abbe Museum, Eindhoven, The Netherlands

SELECTED GROUP EXHIBITIONS

1966	The Jewish Museum, New York, "Primary Structures: Younger American and British Sculptors"
1967	Los Angeles County Museum of Art, "American Sculpture of the Sixties" (traveled)
1968	Haags Gemeentemuseum, The Hague, The Netherlands, "Minimal Art" (traveled)
	Kassel, West Germany, "Documenta 4"
1969	Whitney Museum of American Art, New York, "Anti-Illusion: Procedures/Materials"
1970	The Museum of Modern Art, New York, "Information"
	Whitney Museum of American Art, New York, "1970 Annual Exhibition: Contemporary American Sculpture"
1973	Whitney Museum of American Art, New York, "1973 Biennial Exhibition"
1975	National Collection of Fine Arts, Washington, D.C., "Sculpture: American Directions 1974–75" (traveled)
1976	The Museum of Modern Art, New York, "Drawing Now" (traveled)
1977	Musée National d'Art Moderne, Centre Georges Pompidou, Paris, "Paris—New York"
1978	Stedelijk Museum, Amsterdam, "Made by Sculptors"
1982	The Solomon R. Guggenheim Museum, New York, "The New York School: Four Decades"
	Kassel, West Germany, "Documenta 7"
1983	The Museum of Contemporary Art, Los Angeles, "The First Show: Painting and Sculpture from Eight Collections 1940–1980"

SELECTED BIBLIOGRAPHY

Bourdon, David. *Carl Andre: Sculpture 1959–1977*. New York: Jaap Rietman, Inc., 1978. Foreword by Barbara Rose.

de Jonge, Piet. *Carl Andre* (exhibition catalogue). The Hague, The Netherlands: Haags Gemeentemuseum; Eidenhoven, The Netherlands: Stedelijk van Abbemuseum, 1987.

Gachnang, Johannes, ed. *Carl Andre: Sculpture 1958–1974* (exhibition catalogue). Bern, Switzerland: Kunsthalle Bern, 1975.

McShine, Kynaston L. *Primary Structures: Younger American and British Sculptors* (exhibition catalogue). New York: The Jewish Museum, 1966.

Waldman, Diane. *Carl Andre* (exhibition catalogue). New York: The Solomon R. Guggenheim Museum, 1970.

Mel **Bochner**

Perception of an object is generally pre-conceived as taking place within a point by point time. This disconnected time, a lingering bias of tense in language, restricts our experiencing the conjunction between object and observation. When this conjunction is acknowledged, "things" become indistinguishable from events. Carried to its conclusion, physicality, or what separates the material from the non-material (the object from our observation), is merely a contextual detail.

A structure that concerns the non-object oriented artist is the language which he uses to formulate his thoughts. There is nothing inherently anti-visual about this pursuit. Works of art are not illustrations of ideas....All art exists as it exists within its own described set of conditions. The only esthetic question is recognition...re-cognition...thinking it again.

Mel Bochner, "Excerpts from Speculation (1967-1970)," *Artforum*, 8 (May 1970), pp. 70-71.

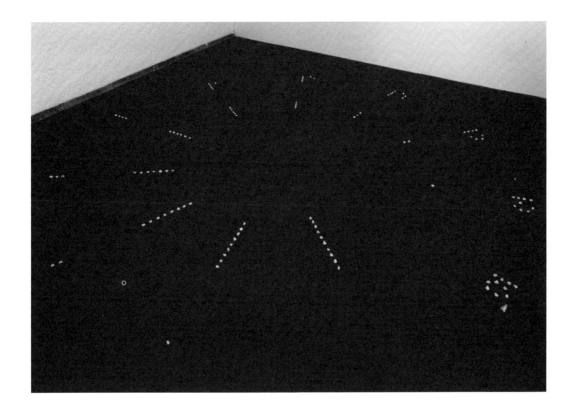

Ten to 10, 1972

Stones, 120 inches diameter

Whitney Museum of American Art, New York;

Purchase, with funds from the Gilman Foundation, Inc.   77.28

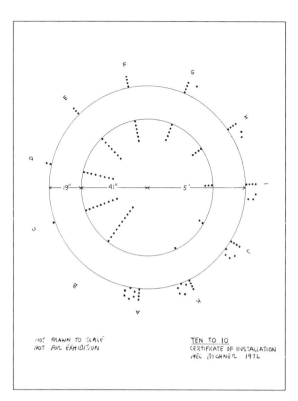

19" 41" 5'

NOT DRAWN TO SCALE
NOT FOR EXHIBITION

TEN TO 10
CERTIFICATE OF INSTALLATION
MEL BOCHNER 1972

Mel Bochner

TEN TO 10

1972

Installation Procedures:

Material: 110 small pebbles
Tools: string, nail, chalk, tapemeasure, protractor

1. Choose a 20' x 20' floor area which offers access from all sides.
   The diameter of the sculpture is 10'.

2. Find the center of this area and insert a nail (or other device to
   hold string) firmly.

3. Tie a string to the center point, pull taut and mark two references
   on the string; a.) 41" from the center, b.) 5' from the center.
   Use the string both for measurement and as a device to line up the
   pebbles. It is unnecessary to draw any line on the floor.

4. Select as a starting point the pebble most immediately accessible to
   the viewer. It will lie 5' from the center, 10" to the left of a line
   parallel to the wall.

WALL   WALL

← LINE PARALLEL
  TO WALL

Note: Station A,
(the 10) should be
"upsidedown" to the
viewer when they
first encounter
the sculpture.

WALL

Note: diagrams
not drawn to scale.

2.

Then layout, as indicated in the initial drawing, station A, ten pebbles
to form the numeral 10 (to be read from the center of the work). The 0
is formed by six pebbles at the points of a regular hexagon,

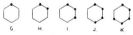

which will read as 0 in context. The axis of the 0 is not parallel to
the 1, but must point towards the center.

center

The angle between the
axes of the 1 and the
0 is approx. 5°

5. With the protractor measure an angle of 33° and then rotate string to
   station B. Beginning 41" from the center set down a line of ten
   pebbles about 17" in length. The actual length of the line is determined by the pebbles, which should always appear to be uniformly spaced
   at about one pebble distance apart. It decreases by 2" at each station.

6. Continuing around the circle, the angle between all radial lines remains
   33°. The next four stations - C through F - each consist of an inner
   row of pebbles starting at 41" and an outer row starting at 5' and
   moving away from the center. The inner line decreases by one pebble
   at each station, while the outer line increases by one, so that there
   are always ten pebbles at each station.

7. For the ramaining five radii - G through K - the inner line continues
   to decrease, while the numeral 10 is sequentially formed on the outer
   circumference. The 0 takes shape by the addition of one pebble per
   station in a clockwise rotation from the top.

   G.   H.   I.   J.   K.

The bottom pebble of the 0 (at stations J, K, and A) touches the
circumference of the outer circle 5' from the center.

8. The final station is also the starting point A. No pebbles remain
   along the inner line and the complete numeral 10 has been formed
   by the ten pebbles.

3.

9. Check to be sure all pebbles look evenly spaced and are in straight
   lines (use string). Carefully mark the final positions beneath each
   pebble with chalk or crayon so that they can be replaced precisely.
   Do not glue. Adhere lightly with bulletin-board wax or something
   similar. The wax will keep the pebbles from drifting yet permit
   removal and reuse.

10. Remove center point and string.

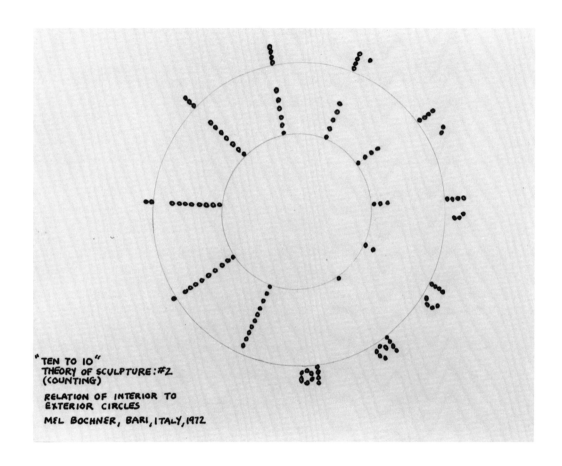

"Ten to 10" Theory of Sculpture: #2 (Counting) —

Relation of Interior to Exterior Circles, 1972

Ink and graphite on paper, 7 1/2 x 9 3/4 inches

Collection of Mrs. Victor W. Ganz

Five and Fifth, 1972

Stones and chalk on floor, dimensions variable

Sonnabend Gallery, New York

Born in Pittsburgh, 1940
Studied at Carnegie Institute of Technology, Pittsburgh
(B.F.A., 1962); Northwestern University, Evanston, Illinois (1963)
Lives in New York

SELECTED ONE-ARTIST EXHIBITIONS

1966   Visual Arts Gallery, School of Visual Arts, New York
1969   Ace Gallery, Los Angeles
        Galerie Konrad Fischer, Düsseldorf
        Galerie Heiner Friedrich, Munich
1970   Galleria Sperone, Turin, Italy
1971   The Museum of Modern Art, New York
1972   Sonnabend Gallery, New York
1974   University Art Museum, University of California, Berkeley
1975   Galerie Ricke, Cologne
1976   The Baltimore Museum of Art
1978   Galerie Sonnabend, Paris
        Sonnabend Gallery, New York
        Daniel Weinberg Gallery, San Francisco
1980   Sonnabend Gallery, New York
1981   Daniel Weinberg Gallery, San Francisco
1982   Sonnabend Gallery, New York
        Centre Internationale de Création Artistique, Abbaye de
        Sénanque, Gordes, France
1983   Sonnabend Gallery, New York
        Daniel Weinberg Gallery, San Francisco
1985   Carnegie-Mellon University Art Gallery, Pittsburgh
1986   Kunstmuseum Luzern, Switzerland
1987   Center for the Fine Arts, Miami
        Sonnabend Gallery, New York

SELECTED GROUP EXHIBITIONS

1969   Kunsthalle Bern, Switzerland, "Live in your head:
        When Attitudes Become Form" (Works—Concepts—
        Processes—Situations—Information) (traveled)

        Museum of Contemporary Art, Chicago, "Art by Telephone"
1970   Galleria d'Arte Moderna, Turin, Italy, "Conceptual
        Art/Arte Povera/Land Art"
        The Museum of Modern Art, New York, "Information"
1972   Kassel, West Germany, "Documenta 5"
1974   The Art Museum, Princeton Univeristy, New Jersey,
        "Line as Language: Six Artists Draw"
1975   Contemporary Arts Center, Cincinnati, "Mel Bochner,
        Barry Le Va, Dorothea Rockburne, Richard Tuttle"
1976   The Art Institute of Chicago, "72nd American Exhibition"
        The Museum of Modern Art, New York, "Drawing Now"
        (traveled)
1977   Whitney Museum of American Art, New York, "1977
        Biennial Exhibition"
1978   Philadelphia Museum of Art, "Eight Artists"
1979   Palazzo Reale, Milan, "Pittura Ambiente"
        Whitney Museum of American Art, New York, "1979
        Biennial Exhibition"
1980   Hayden Gallery, Massachusetts Institute of Technology,
        Cambridge, "Mel Bochner/Richard Serra"
1982   The Art Institue of Chicago, "74th American Exhibition"
1987   Institute of Contemporary Art, University of Pennsylvania,
        Philadelphia, "1967: At the Crossroads"

SELECTED BIBLIOGRAPHY

Halbreich, Kathy. *Mel Bochner/Richard Serra* (exhibition
        catalogue). Cambridge, Massachusetts: Hayden Gallery,
        Massachusetts Institute of Technology, 1980.
King, Elaine A. *Mel Bochner: 1973–1985* (exhibition catalogue).
        Pittsburgh: Carnegie-Mellon University Art Gallery, 1985.
Pincus-Witten, Robert. "Mel Bochner: The Constant as Variable."
        Artforum, 11 (December 1972), pp. 28-34.
Richardson, Brenda. *Mel Bochner: Number and Shape* (exhibition
        catalogue). Baltimore: The Baltimore Museum of Art, 1976.
Watkins, Ragland, ed. *Mel Bochner, Barry LeVa, Dorothea Rockburne,
        Richard Tuttle* (exhibition catalogue). Cincinnati:
        Contemporary Arts Center, 1975.

Jonathan **Borofsky**

Running People at 2,616,216 *is an image that has always been rather strong for me. It looks primitive—like it could have been in a cave—and it also looks fairly contemporary. The original drawing was on the same page that also included the drawing for* Hammering Man *and was done in 1976. Around 1978, I was going through these earlier scribbles, and I remember thinking that it looked pretty good. I then took them to a photography studio and had them enlarged to 8 by 10 inch photographs from the original stamp-size images. I then had them made into transparencies and started projecting them directly on the wall. The figures start out being kind of chaotic—with the figures jumping around a little and then slowly running towards the right. This image starts off flaky and jumpy and moves right into people running, with a little more clarity with each figure.*

Jonathan Borofsky, from an interview with Richard Marshall, July 7, 1983.

Running People at 2,616,216, 1979

Latex paint on wall, dimensions variable

Whitney Museum of American Art, New York; Purchase,

with funds from the Painting and Sculpture Committee   84.43

Installation at Kunsthalle Basel, Switzerland, 1981.

Installation **Instructions**

Use black latex house paint thin enough to flow evenly.
Regular paint brushes are much too slow for this task. Use
2" sponge brushes....These sponge brushes make clean
lines on the wall and the work fast. The problem is they
loose their elasticity after about 10 minutes working time so
be prepared to use at least 20 to 30 sponge brushes for one
very large painting. Fill in the large areas with a 3" roller.

   The piece looks best when painted large and bold
20-40 feet long across walls and maybe ceiling.

   Using the projected transparency, trace its outer
edges carefully with the sponge brushes and then fill in
using brush (or roller for large areas). These brushes, unlike
bristle brushes, make long clean lines across walls very
easily. All the original white areas must be left in the
painting.

   The bottom horizontal lines are usually used to
add to the feeling of motion and landscape. I have almost
never used the top horizontal lines and I recommend
against it. These 4 long lines at the bottom can be easily and
smoothly painted with the sponge brushes.

   The *Running People* look best going from left to
right, but can go the other way if necessary.

   The painting of *Running People* is an exercise in
tracing the outer edges and then filling it in. If the painting is
done with some assertiveness, a 30 foot image can be
painted in about 4-5 hours.

Running People at 2,616,216, 1979

Installation at Whitney Museum of American Art,

New York, 1989.

Running People at 2,616,216, 1979

Installation at Paula Cooper Gallery, New York, 1980.

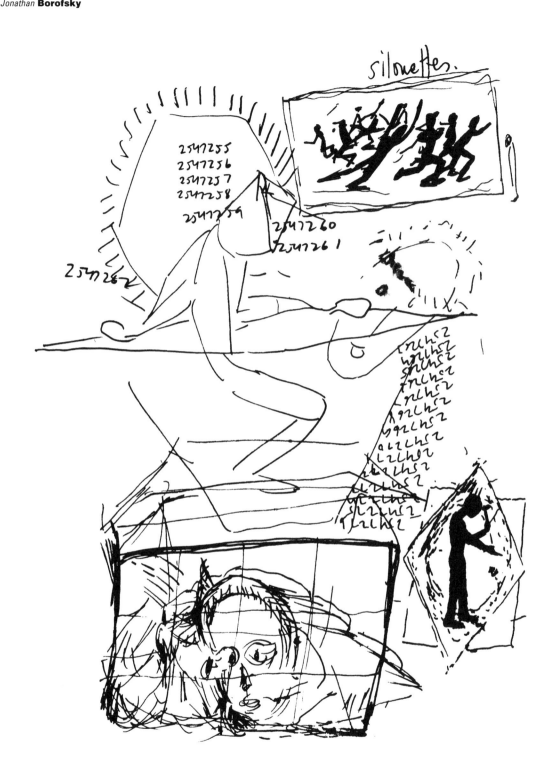

*Many of my large images originated as small doodles or mindless
scribbles—like when I'm on the telephone at 2,547,255 to 2,547,276*, 1976
Ink on paper, 11 x 8 1/2 inches   Kunstmuseum Basel, Switzerland

Born in Boston, 1942

Studied at Carnegie-Mellon University, Pittsburgh (B.F.A., 1964); École de Fontainebleau (1964); Yale University, New Haven (M.F.A., 1966)

Lives in Venice, California

SELECTED ONE-ARTIST EXHIBITIONS

1975   Paula Cooper Gallery, New York

1976   Wadsworth Atheneum, Hartford

1977   Fine Art Gallery, University of California, Irvine

1978   Corps de Garde, Groningen, The Netherlands

        The Museum of Modern Art, New York

        University Art Museum, University of California, Berkeley

1979   InK. (Halle für Internationale neue Kunst), Zurich

        Portland Center for the Visual Arts, Oregon

1980   Paula Cooper Gallery, New York

1981   Institute of Contemporary Arts, London

        Kunsthalle Basel, Switzerland

1982   Paula Cooper Gallery, New York

        Museum Boymans-van Beuningen, Rotterdam

        Museum van Hedendaagse Kunst, Ghent, Belgium

1983   Kunstmuseum Basel, Switzerland

        Paula Cooper Gallery, New York

1984   Moderna Museet, Stockholm

        Philadelphia Museum of Art and Whitney Museum of American Art, New York (traveled)

1987   Tokyo Metropolitan Art Museum (traveled)

1988   Paula Cooper Gallery, New York

SELECTED GROUP EXHIBITIONS

1969   Paula Cooper Gallery, New York, "No. 7"

1975   Whitney Museum of American Art, Downtown Branch, New York, "Autogeography"

1976   Akademie der Künste, Berlin, "New York—Downtown Manhattan: SoHo"

        Venice, Italy, "37th Biennale di Venezia"

1979   Neuberger Museum, State University of New York at Purchase, "Ten Artists/Artists Space"

        Whitney Museum of American Art, New York, "1979 Biennial Exhibition"

1980   Venice, Italy, "39th Biennale di Venezia"

1981   Musée National d'Art Moderne, Centre Georges Pompidou, Paris, "Murs"

1982   Kassel, West Germany, "Documenta 7"

        Martin-Gropius-Bau, West Berlin, "Zeitgeist"

        Walker Art Center, Minneapolis, "Eight Artists: The Anxious Edge"

1983   Tate Gallery, London, "New Art"

        Whitney Museum of American Art, New York, "1983 Biennial Exhibition"

1985   Museum of Art, Carnegie Institute, Pittsburgh, "1985 Carnegie International"

1986   The Art Institute of Chicago, "75th American Exhibition"

        The Museum of Contemporary Art, Los Angeles, "The Barry Lowen Collection"

1987   The Museum of Modern Art, New York, "BERLINART 1961–1987"

SELECTED BIBLIOGRAPHY

Geelhaar, Christian, and Dieter Koepplin. *Jonathan Borofsky: Zeichnungen 1960-1983* (exhibition catalogue). Basel, Switzerland: Kunstmuseum Basel, 1983.

Marshall, Richard, and Jean-Christophe Amman. *Jonathan Borofsky* (exhibition catalogue). Tokyo: Metropolitan Art Museum, 1987.

Rosenthal, Mark, and Richard Marshall. *Jonathan Borofsky* (exhibition catalogue). Philadelphia: Philadelphia Museum of Art in association with the Whitney Museum of American Art, 1984.

Simon, Joan. "An Interview with Jonathan Borofsky," *Art in America*, 69 (November 1981), pp. 156-167.

Dan **Flavin**

The pink, yellow and red [for] Robert...*has a rich contrast,
front over rear, and an optical interplay, pink on yellow back-
grounded by the red, all modified by reflected color mixes
and shadows of the grid structure itself. As an ensemble, this
intense fluorescent light use/abuse seems to me to be rare in
my production.*

Dan Flavin, statement dated May 4, 1978, Artists' Files, Whitney Museum of
American Art, New York.

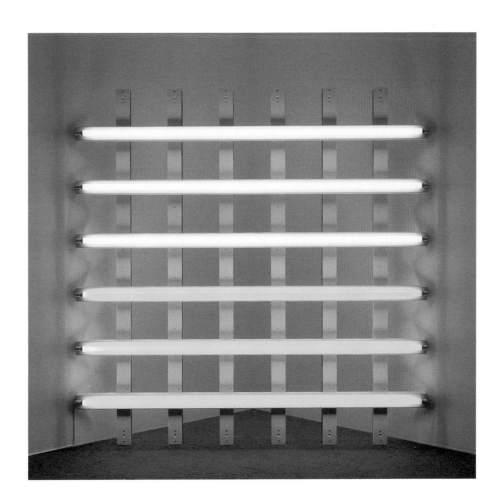

Untitled (for Robert with fond regards), 1977

Pink, yellow, and red fluorescent lights, 96 x 96 inches across the corner

Whitney Museum of American Art, New York; Purchase, with funds from the

Louis and Bessie Adler Foundation, Inc., Seymour M. Klein, President, the

Howard and Jean Lipman Foundation, Inc., by exchange, and gift of Peter M.

Brant, by exchange   78.57

I came to these conclusions about what I had found in fluores-cent light, and about what might be done with it plastically: Now the entire spatial container and its parts — wall, floor, ceiling — could support this strip of light but would not restrict its act of light except to unfold it. Regard the light and you are fascinated — inhibited from grasping its limits at each end. While the tube itself has an actual length of eight feet, its shadow, cast by the supporting pan, has none but an illusion dissolving at its ends. This waning shadow cannot really be measured without resisting its visual effect and breaking the poetry. Realizing this, I knew that the actual space of a room could be broken down and played with by planting illusions of real light (electric light) at crucial junctures in the room's composition.

Dan Flavin, "'...in daylight or cool white':an autobiographical sketch," *Artforum*, 4 (December 1965), p. 24.

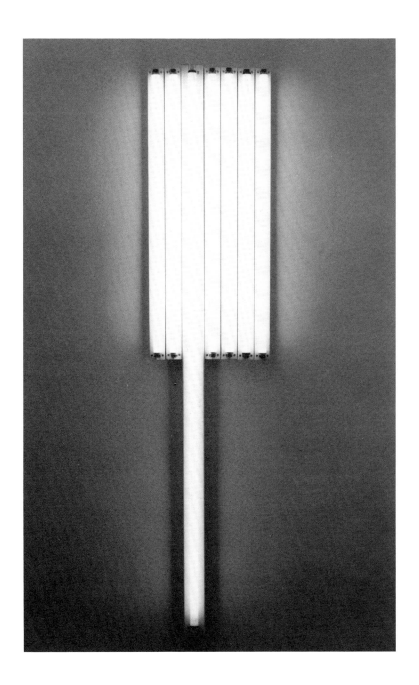

Untitled, 1966

White fluorescent lights, 96 x 21 x 3 1/2 inches

Whitney Museum of American Art, New York;

Gift of Howard and Jean Lipman   71.214

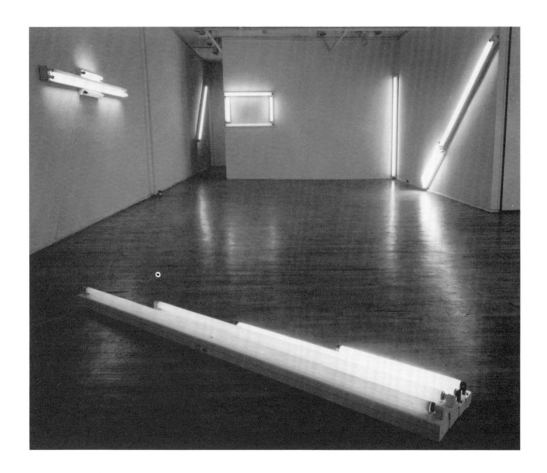

Installation view, Green Gallery, New York, 1964.

Born in New York, 1933

Studied at The New School for Social Research, New York (1956);

Columbia University, New York (1957-59)

Lives in Garrison, New York

SELECTED ONE-ARTIST EXHIBITIONS

1961	Hudson Gallery, New York
1964	Green Gallery, New York
1966	Museum of Contemporary Art, Chicago
	Galerie Rudolf Zwirner, Cologne
1968	Dwan Gallery, New York
	Galerie Heiner Friedrich, Munich
1969	National Gallery of Canada, Ottawa
	The Jewish Museum, New York
	Los Angeles County Museum of Art
1971	John Weber Gallery, New York
1975	Fort Worth Art Museum
1976	Portland Center for the Visual Arts, Oregon
1977	The Art Institute of Chicago
1978	University Art Museum, University of California, Berkeley
1979	The Hudson River Museum, Yonkers, New York (traveled)
1981	Leo Castelli Gallery, New York
1982	The Solomon R. Guggenheim Museum, New York
1984	The Corcoran Gallery of Art, Washington, D.C.
	The Museum of Contemporary Art, Los Angeles
1985	CAPC Musée d'art Contemporaine, Bordeaux, France
	Rijksmuseum Kröller-Müller, Otterlo, The Netherlands
1986	Arthur M. Sackler Museum, Harvard University, Cambridge, Massachusetts

SELECTED GROUP EXHIBITIONS

1965	Green Gallery, New York, "Flavin/Judd/Morris/Williams"
1966	The Jewish Museum, New York, "Primary Structures: Younger American and British Sculptors"
1968	Kassel, West Germany, "Documenta 4"
1969	The Metropolitan Museum of Art, New York, "New York Painting and Sculpture: 1940-1970"
1970	The Museum of Modern Art, New York, "Spaces"
	Whitney Museum of American Art, New York, "1970 Annual Exhibition: Contemporary American Sculpture"
1971	Walker Art Center, Minneapolis, "Works for New Spaces"
1972	The Art Institute of Chicago, "70th American Exhibition"
1976	The Museum of Modern Art, New York, "Drawing Now" (traveled)
	Whitney Museum of American Art, New York, "200 Years of American Sculpture"
1979	Institute of Contemporary Art, Boston, "The Reductive Object: A Survey of the Minimalist Aesthetic in the 1960s"
	Whitney Museum of American Art, New York, "The Decade in Review: Selections from the 1970s"
1980	InK. (Halle für Internationale neue Kunst), Zurich, "Hauptwerke der Minimal Art"
1984	Whitney Museum of American Art, New York, "Blam! The Explosion of Pop, Minimalism, and Performance 1958-1964"
1985	CAPC Musée d'Art Contemporain, Bordeaux, France, "Art Minimal I"

SELECTED BIBLIOGRAPHY

Belloli, Jay and Emily S. Rauh. *Dan Flavin: Drawings, Diagrams and Prints 1972–1975* (exhibition catalogue). Fort Worth: Fort Worth Art Museum, 1977.

Flavin, Dan. *Drawn Along the Shores 1959–1976* (exhibition catalogue). Yonkers, New York: The Hudson River Museum, 1979.

Geldzahler, Henry. *New York Painting and Sculpture: 1940–1970* (exhibition catalogue). New York: The Metropolitan Museum of Art, 1969.

Smith, Brydon. *Dan Flavin, Fluorescent Light Etc.* (exhibition catalogue). Ottawa: National Gallery of Canada, 1969.

Robert **Irwin**

*The question for the discs was very simple....How do I paint a
painting that doesn't begin and end at the edge? In other words,
I no longer felt comfortable with that sense of confinement....
Still, in the beginning it was a simple artistic challenge: How do
I paint a painting that does not begin and end at an edge but
rather starts to take in and become involved with the space or
environment around it?....The reason for the circular disc...
as opposed to making them square, was that that eliminated
the four corners, corners being really powerful focal points,
whereas what I was after was an evenness of presence....The
circle was simply the most neutral shape I could find....Visually
it was very ambiguous which was more real, the object or
its shadow. They were basically equal. I mean, they occupied
space very differently, but there was no separation in terms of
your visual acuity in determining that one was more real
than the other. And that was the real beauty of those things,
that they achieved a balance between space occupied and
unoccupied in which both became intensely occupied at the
level of perceptual energy....the discs resolved that one
simple question—how to paint a painting that doesn't begin or
end at the edge—by more or less transcending painting....
After the discs...there was no reason for me to go on being a
painter....When I married the painting to the environment,
suddenly it had to deal with the environment around it as being
equal to the figure and having as much meaning.*

Quoted in Lawrence Weschler, *Seeing is Forgetting The Name of the Thing One
Sees* (Berkeley and Los Angeles: University of California Press, 1982), pp. 99-109.

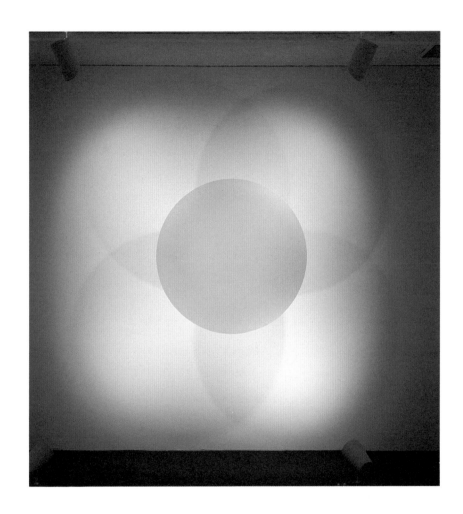

No Title, 1966–67

Acrylic on aluminum with four electric lights,

48 inches diameter x 13 inches deep

Whitney Museum of American Art, New York;

Purchase, with funds from the Howard and

Jean Lipman Foundation, Inc.   68.42

Scrim Veil—Black Rectangle—Natural Light, Whitney Museum of American Art, New York, 1977

Cloth, metal, and wood, 12 x 114 x 49 feet

Whitney Museum of American Art, New York; Gift of the artist   77.45

*Scrim Veil—Black Rectangle—Natural Light, Whitney Museum of American
Art, New York,* 1977

Cloth, metal, and wood, 12 x 114 x 49 feet

Whitney Museum of American Art, New York; Gift of the artist   77.45

Installation **Instructions**

Piece is installed on a wall 15 to 18 feet wide.

Floor spotlights are placed approximately 5 feet from back wall, and 15 to 18 feet apart; upper spotlights must also be approximately 5 feet from back wall.

Distance from floor to center of piece should equal distance from center of piece to upper spotlights.

Wall must be white or off-white.

Born in Long Beach, California, 1928

Studied at Otis Art Institute, Los Angeles (1948-50); Jepson Art Institute, Los Angeles (1951); Chouinard Art Institute, Los Angeles (1952-54)

Lives in San Diego, California

SELECTED ONE-ARTIST EXHIBITIONS

1957	Felix Landau Gallery, Los Angeles
1959	Ferus Gallery, Los Angeles
1960	Pasadena Art Museum, California
1966	The Pace Gallery, New York
1968	Pasadena Art Museum, California
1969	La Jolla Museum of Contemporary Art, California
1970	The Museum of Modern Art, New York
1972	Fogg Art Museum, Harvard University, Cambridge, Massachusetts
	Mizuno Gallery, Los Angeles
1975	Fort Worth Art Museum
	Museum of Contemporary Art, Chicago
1976	Walker Art Center, Minneapolis
1977	Whitney Museum of American Art, New York
1979	University Art Museum, University of California, Berkeley
1982	Louisiana Museum of Art, Humlebaeck, Denmark
1984	San Francisco Museum of Modern Art
1987	Wave Hill, Bronx, New York

SELECTED GROUP EXHIBITONS

1952	Los Angeles County Museum of Art, "Annual Exhibition—Artists of Los Angeles and Vicinity"
1957	Whitney Museum of American Art, New York, "1957 Annual Exhibition: Contemporary American Sculpture, Paintings, and Watercolors"
1962	Whitney Museum of American Art, New York, "Fifty California Artists" (traveled)
1964	Sidney Janis Gallery, New York, "Seven New Artists"
1965	The Museum of Modern Art, New York, "The Responsive Eye" (traveled)
1966	Los Angeles County Museum of Art, "Robert Irwin/ Kenneth Price"
1968	Kassel, West Germany, "Documenta 4"
1969	Fort Worth Art Center, "Robert Irwin/Doug Wheeler" (traveled)
	Pasadena Art Museum, California, "West Coast 1945–1969" (traveled)
1970	The Art Institute of Chicago, "69th American Exhibition"
	Tate Gallery, London, "Bell/Irwin/Wheeler"
1971	Hayward Gallery, London, "11 Los Angeles Artists"
	Los Angeles County Museum of Art, "Art and Technology"
	Walker Art Center, Minneapolis, "Works for New Spaces"
1976	Fine Arts Center Gallery, University of Massachusetts, Amherst, "Critical Perspective in American Art"
1979	University Art Museum, University of California, Berkeley, "Andre/Buren/Irwin/Nordman: Space as Support"
1981	Los Angeles County Museum of Art, "Seventeen Artists of the Sixties"

SELECTED BIBLIOGRAPHY

Licht, Ira. *Robert Irwin* (exhibition catalogue). Chicago: Museum of Contemporary Art, 1975.

Marshall, Richard, ed. *Robert Irwin* (exhibition catalogue). New York: Whitney Museum of American Art, 1977. Essay by Robert Irwin.

Rosenthal, Mark. *Andre/Buren/Irwin/Nordman: Space as Support* (exhibition catalogue). Berkeley: University Art Museum, University of California, Berkeley, 1979.

Tuchman, Maurice, ed. *Robert Irwin/Kenneth Price* (exhibition catalogue). Los Angeles, Los Angeles County Museum of Art, 1966.

Weschler, Lawrence. *Seeing is Forgetting the Name of the Thing One Sees: The Life of Contemporary Artist Robert Irwin.* Berkeley and Los Angeles: University of California Press, 1982.

Sol **LeWitt**

I wanted to do a work of art that was as two-dimensional as possible. It seems more natural to work directly on walls than to make a construction, to work on that, and then put the construction on the wall. The physical properties of the wall: height, length, color, material, and architectural conditions and intrusions, are a necessary part of the wall drawings. Different kinds of walls make for different kinds of drawings. Imperfections on the wall surface are occasionally apparent after the drawing is completed. These should be considered a part of the wall drawing....The wall drawing is a permanent installation, until destroyed. Once something is done, it cannot be undone.

Sol LeWitt, "Wall Drawings," in Gregory Battock, "Documentation in Conceptual Art," *Arts Magagzine*, 44 (April 1970), p. 45.

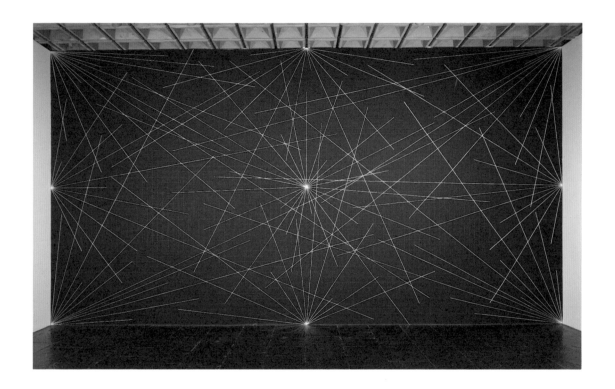

*Lines to Points on a Six Inch Grid. 4th wall: 24 lines from the center, 12 lines
from the midpoint of each of the sides, 12 lines from each corner*, 1976
White crayon lines and black pencil grid on black walls, dimensions variable
Whitney Museum of American Art, New York;
Purchase, with funds from the Gilman Foundation, Inc.   78.1.1-4

C E R T I F I C A T E

This is to certify that the Sol LeWitt wall drawing
number ___289___ evidenced by this certificate is authentic.

```
A six-inch (15 cm) grid covering each of the four
black walls.  White lines to points on the grids.
1st wall:  24 lines from the center;
2nd wall:  12 lines from the midpoint of each of
                the sides;
3rd wall:  12 lines from each corner;
4th wall:  24 lines from the center, 12 lines from
                the midpoint of each of the sides, 12
                lines from each corner.
(The length of the lines and their placement are
determined by the draftsman.)

White crayon lines, black pencil grid, black walls
First Drawn by:  Jo Watanabe
First Installation:  Detroit Institute of Arts,
                Detroit, MI.  July, 1976
First Installation 4th wall:  Museum of Modern Art,
                New York, NY.
                January, 1976
First Drawn by:  Jo Watanabe, Ryo Watanabe
```

This certification is the signature for the wall drawing and must

accompany the wall drawing if it is sold or otherwise transferred.

Certified by _____

Sol LeWitt

D I A G R A M

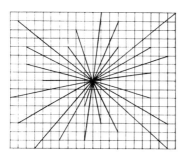

This is a diagram for the Sol LeWitt wall drawing number *289 ¹/₄* . It should accompany the certificate if the wall drawing is sold or otherwise transferred but is not a certificate or a drawing.

D I A G R A M

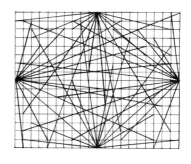

This is a diagram for the Sol LeWitt wall drawing number *289 ²/₄*. It should accompany the certificate if the wall drawing is sold or otherwise transferred but is not a certificate or a drawing.

D I A G R A M

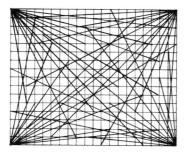

This is a diagram for the Sol LeWitt wall drawing number *289 ³/₄*. It should accompany the certificate if the wall drawing is sold or otherwise transferred but is not a certificate or a drawing.

D I A G R A M

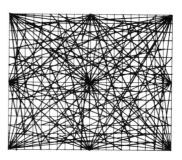

This is a diagram for the Sol LeWitt wall drawing number *289 ⁴/₄* It should accompany the certificate if the wall drawing is sold or otherwise transferred but is not a certificate or a drawing.

Lines to Points on a Six Inch Grid, 1976

Installation views

Born in Hartford, Connecticut, 1928
Studied at Syracuse University, New York (B.F.A., 1949)
Lives in Chester, Connecticut

SELECTED ONE-ARTIST EXHIBITIONS

1965	Daniels Gallery, New York
1966	Dwan Gallery, New York
1968	Galerie Konrad Fischer, Düsseldorf
1969	Museum Haus Lange, Krefeld, West Germany
1971	John Weber Gallery, New York
1973	Museum of Modern Art, Oxford, England
	Portland Center for the Visual Arts, Oregon
1974	Stedelijk Museum, Amsterdam
	John Weber Gallery, New York
1975	Kunsthalle Basel, Switzerland
1977	University Gallery, University of Massachusetts, Amherst
1978	The Museum of Modern Art, New York (traveled)
1979	InK. (Halle für Internationale neue Kunst), Zurich
	Margo Leavin Gallery, Los Angeles
1980	Texas Gallery, Houston
1981	Galerie Yvon Lambert, Paris
	Wadsworth Atheneum, Hartford
1982	John Weber Gallery, New York
1985	Haags Gemeentemuseum, The Hague, The Netherlands
1986	John Weber Gallery, New York

SELECTED GROUP EXHIBITIONS

1966	Finch College Museum of Art, New York, "Art in Process"
	The Jewish Museum, New York, "Primary Structures: Younger American and British Sculptors"
1967	Los Angeles County Museum of Art, "American Sculpture of the Sixties"
1968	The Museum of Modern Art, New York, "Art of the Real" (traveled)
1969	Kunsthalle Bern, Switzerland, "Live in Your Head: When Attitudes Become Form (Works—Concepts—Processes—Situations—Information" (traveled)
1970	The Museum of Modern Art, New York, "Information"
1972	Institute of Contemporary Art, University of Pennsylvania, Philadelphia, "Grids"
1974	The Art Museum, Princeton University, New Jersey, "Line as Language: Six Artists Draw"
1976	Whitney Museum of American Art, New York, "200 Years of American Sculpture"
1977	Kassel, West Germany, "Documenta 6"
1979	The Art Institute of Chicago, "73rd American Exhibition"
	Whitney Museum of American Art, New York, "1979 Biennial Exhibition"
1982	The Art Institute of Chicago, "74th American Exhibition"
	Kassel, West Germany, "Documenta 7"
1983	The Museum of Contemporary Art, Los Angeles, "The First Show: Painting and Sculpture from Eight Collections, 1940–1980"
1987	Whitney Museum of American Art, New York "1987 Biennial Exhibition"

SELECTED BIBLIOGRAPHY

Legg, Alicia, ed. *Sol LeWitt* (exhibition catalogue). New York: The Museum of Modern Art, 1978.

LeWitt, Sol. *Incomplete Open Cubes* (exhibition catalogue). New York: John Weber Gallery, 1974.

McShine, Kynaston L. *Primary Structures: Younger American and British Sculptors* (exhibition catalogue). New York: The Jewish Museum, 1966.

Singer, Susanna, ed. *Sol LeWitt Wall Drawings 1968–1984* (exhibition catalogue). Amsterdam: Stedelijk Museum, 1984.

Wember, Paul. *Sol LeWitt: Sculptures and Wall Drawings* (exhibition catalogue). Krefeld, West Germany: Museum Haus Lange, 1969.

Mary **Lucier**

This work is an investigation of light in landscape and its function as an agent of memory, both personal and mythic. It deals with the convergence of disparate entities —geographies, periods in time, sensibilities; with transitions from one state of being to another; and how, within the frame of imagination and collective memory, these "dissolves" take place. It is structured as a journey of the camera from rural Ohio to Giverny in France. In this adventure, landscape is the sole protagonist: articulated by changing light and by camera movement, animated by highly pictorial sound, and made poignant by the very absence of inhabitants. References to the motifs of Monet function throughout as the "art historical" memory, underlying the more personal evocation of French and American personae. While a strong subliminal narrative gives the piece a very linear development in time, the alternating spatial deployment of the two tapes across a sweep of seven screens allows a generous exposition of landscape panorama —at once cinematic, sculptural, and theatrical.

Quoted in William Judson, *Mary Lucier: Ohio at Giverny*, exhibition catalogue (Pittsburgh: Museum of Art, Carnegie Institute, 1983), n.p.

Ohio at Giverny, 1983

Video installation: two videotapes, color, sound, 18 1/2 minutes; seven
monitors, progressing in size from left to right, 13 inches, 15 inches, 15 inches,
17 inches, 19 inches, 21 inches, 21 inches; and synchronous starter,
97 x 268 x 198 inches (variable)

Whitney Museum of American Art, New York; Purchase, with funds from the
Louis and Bessie Adler Foundation, Inc., Seymour M. Klein, President, and
Mrs. Rudolph B. Schulhof   83.35a-j

Installation **Instructions**

An installation for two synchronized videotapes displayed on seven television monitors mounted behind a concave wall in such a manner that only the picture screens are visible. The monitors are of progressive screen sizes from 13" to 21" diagonals, increasing left to right along the curve, and are positioned at stepped heights in the wall so as to form an arch or bower at the center. The videotapes, identified as Channel 1 and Channel 2, are shown in alternating sequence across the screens in an A/B/A/B/A/B/A patterning.

The gallery used for this video work should have darkness (i.e. no windows or direct sunlight, or windows, skylights, etc. that can be covered) and should have a corner across which the wall structure can be built. Gallery and structure should be painted white. The soundtrack is an important component of this piece, so gallery should be separate from the other exhibition spaces to allow playing sound at optimum level.

Three different construction plans are available, so the wall may be constructed to fit different exhibition spaces (depending on ceiling height, gallery lay-out, etc.). If necessary, wall can be re-designed to fit a particular space.

The structure consists of two angled panels, one at each side (one of which can accommodate an access door), leading into a gently curving wall composed of seven flat panels of increasing widths arranged at slight angles. Each of these seven panels has a cut-out window to frame a monitor screen, increasing in size from left to right (see diagrams and photographs). Platforms beneath each window at the rear of the wall accommodate the monitors.

The structure should be built across a corner. The space behind the wall can serve as the control room for all the electronic equipment, or the installation can be run remotely from another location in the building. Wall should be constructed of sheetrock or plywood or other material sturdy enough to support the weight of the monitors.

FLOOR PLAN
¼" SCALE

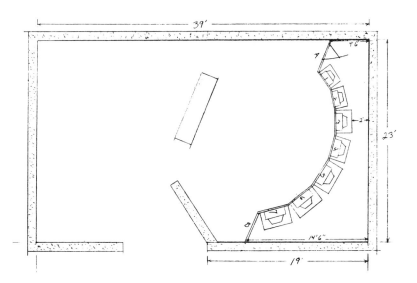

ELEVATION
½" SCALE

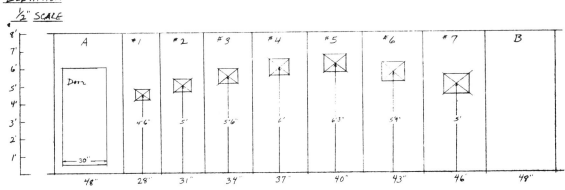

REAR WALL CONSTRUCTION
(NOT TO SCALE)

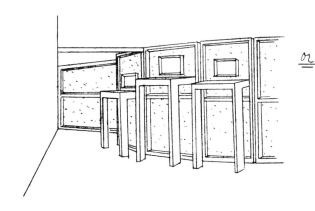

or

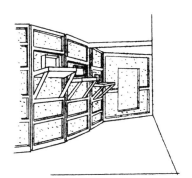

OHIO AT GIVERNY (1983)

Installation plan for
WHITNEY MUSEUM, Lobby
Gallery, October 1986

Mary Lucier 8/11/86

Video stills from *Ohio at Giverny*, 1983.

Born in Bucyrus, Ohio, 1944

Studied at Brandeis University, Waltham, Massachusetts (B.A., 1965)

Lives in New York

SELECTED ONE-ARTIST EXHIBITIONS

1975	The Kitchen, New York
1976	Anthology Film Archives, New York
1978	The Kitchen, New York
1980	The Hudson River Museum, Yonkers, New York
1981	Whitney Museum of American Art, New York
1983	Museum of Art, Carnegie Institute, Pittsburgh
1985	Norton Gallery of Art, West Palm Beach, Florida
1986	The Berkshire Museum, Pittsfield, Massachusetts
	Portland Museum of Art, Maine
	Rose Art Museum, Brandeis University, Waltham, Massachusetts
	Wadsworth Atheneum, Hartford
1987	Neuberger Museum, State University of New York at Purchase
	Dallas Museum of Art
	Madison Art Center, Wisconsin

SELECTED GROUP EXHIBITIONS

1973	The Kitchen, New York, "Red White Yellow and Black"
1974	Rose Art Museum, Brandeis University, Waltham, Massachusetts, "A Generation of Brandeis Artists"
1977	The American Center, Paris, "Art Video USA"
	Musée d'Art Moderne de la Ville de Paris, "10e Biennale de Paris"
1983	The American Film Institute, Los Angeles, "National Video Festival"
	Walter Phillips Gallery, Banff, Canada, "The Second Link—Viewpoints on Video in the Eighties"
	Whitney Museum of American Art, New York, "1983 Biennial Exhibition"

1984	Stedelijk Museum, Amsterdam, "The Luminous Image"
1985	The High Museum of Art, Atlanta, "Atlanta Video Festival"
1986	Katonah Gallery, Katonah, New York, "A Video Primer: Electronic Art from the 1980s"
	Artspace, Sydney, Australia, "New York City Video"
1987	Virginia Museum of Fine Arts, Richmond, "Video Installations: Doug Hall and Mary Lucier"
	Walker Art Center, Minneapolis, "Viewpoints: Paul Kos, Mary Lucier"
	Whitney Museum of American Art, Fairfield County, Stamford, Connecticut, "Contemporary Diptychs: Divided Visions"

SELECTED BIBLIOGRAPHY

Jenkins, Bruce. *Viewpoints: Paul Kos, Mary Lucier* (exhibition brochure). Minneapolis: Walker Art Center, 1987.

Judson, William, and Mary Lucier. *Mary Lucier: Ohio at Giverney* (exhibition catalogue). Pittsburgh: Museum of Art, Carnegie Institute, 1983.

Mignot, Dorine, ed. *The Luminous Image* (exhibition catalogue). Amsterdam: Stedelijk Museum, 1984.

Miller, Nancy. *Wilderness* (exhibition catlaogue). Waltham, Massachusetts: Rose Art Museum, Brandeis University, 1986.

Falk, Loren. *The Second Link* (exhibition catalogue). Banff, Canada: Walter Phillips Gallery, 1983.

Bianchi, Lois. *Video Transformations* (exhibition catalogue). New York: Independent Curators, Inc. 1986.

Bruce **Nauman**

I think in the beginning [my] things were made out of fragile materials, or materials that weren't necessarily art materials, because if I made a piece that was clearly not going to hold up, a lot of preciousness would be removed. Eventually it will fall apart, but the idea is left and could be made over again. The piece may be different but it would still carry the weight of the idea.

Quoted in Coosje Van Bruggen, *Bruce Nauman* (New York: Rizzoli Books, 1988), p. 9.

Untitled, 1965–66

Latex on burlap, 20 x 65 x 40 inches (variable)

Whitney Museum of American Art, New York;

Gift of Mr. and Mrs. Peter M. Brant   76.43

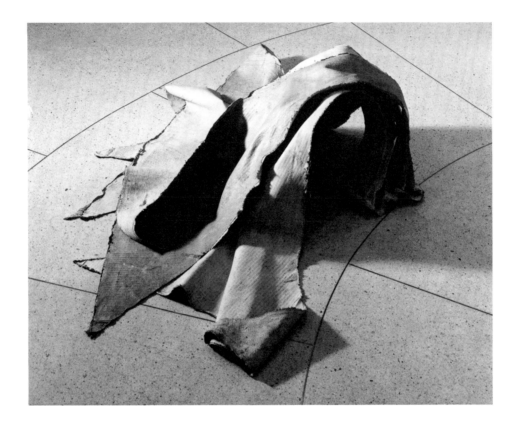

Untitled, 1965–66

Latex on burlap, 20 x 65 x 40 inches (variable)

Whitney Museum of American Art, New York;

Gift of Mr. and Mrs. Peter M. Brant   76.43

Untitled, 1965–66

Cast fiberglass, 54 x 94 x 12 inches

Whitney Museum of American Art, New York;

Gift of Mr. and Mrs. Eugene M. Schwartz   70.1597

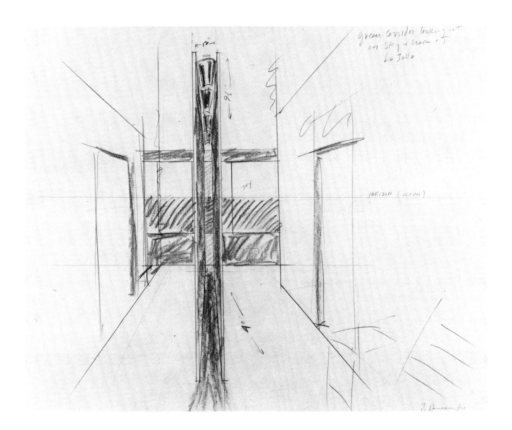

Green Corridor looking out on Sky and Ocean at La Jolla, 1971

Graphite and pastel on paper, 23 x 29 inches

Whitney Museum of American Art, New York;

Gift of Norman Dubrow   77.102

Born in Fort Wayne, Indiana, 1941

Studied at the University of Wisconsin, Madison (B.S., 1964);

University of California, Davis (M.A., 1966)

Lives in Pecos, New Mexico

SELECTED ONE-ARTIST EXHIBITIONS

1966   Nicholas Wilder Gallery, Los Angeles

1968   Leo Castelli Gallery, New York

1969   Galerie Sonnabend, Paris

1971   Helman Gallery, St. Louis

1972   Los Angeles County Museum of Art (traveled)

1975   Albright-Knox Art Gallery, Buffalo

1979   Portland Center for the Visual Arts, Oregon

1981   Rijksmuseum Kröller-Müller, Otterlo, The Netherlands
        (traveled)

1982   The Baltimore Museum of Art

1984   Leo Castelli Gallery, New York

1986   Whitechapel Art Gallery, London (traveled)

1987   Daniel Weinberg Gallery, Los Angeles

1988   Sperone Westwater Gallery, New York

SELECTED GROUP EXHIBITIONS

1967   Los Angeles County Museum of Art, "American Sculpture
        of the Sixties" (traveled)

1969   Kunsthalle Bern, Switzerland, "Live in Your Head:
        When Attitudes Become Form (Works—Concepts—
        Processes—Situations—Information)" (traveled)
        Whitney Museum of American Art, New York, "Anti-
        Illusion: Procedures/Materials"

1970   The Museum of Modern Art, New York, "Information"

1975   Museum of Contemporary Art, Chicago, "Bodyworks"

1976   San Francisco Museum of Modern Art, "Painting and
        Sculpture in California: The Modern Era" (traveled)

1979   Museum Bochum, West Germany, "Words Words"
        (traveled)

1981   Los Angeles County Museum of Art, "Art in Los Angeles—
        Seventeen Artists in the Sixties"

1982   Stedelijk Museum, Amsterdam, "'60–'80: Attitudes/
        Concepts/Images"

1985   The Museum of Modern Art, New York, "New Work on
        Paper 3"

1986   Kunsthalle Basel, Switzerland, "Franz Gertsch and Bruce
        Nauman"

SELECTED BIBLIOGRAPHY

Livingston, Jane, and Marcia Tucker. *Bruce Nauman: Works
        from 1965 to 1972* (exhibition catalogue). Los Angeles:
        Los Angeles County Museum of Art; New York: Whitney
        Museum of American Art, 1972.

Pincus-Witten, Robert. "New York: Bruce Nauman." *Artforum*, 6
        (April 1968), pp. 63-64.

_____."Bruce Nauman: Another Kind of Reasoning." *Artforum*, 10
        (February 1972), pp. 30-37.

Richardson, Brenda. *Bruce Nauman: Neons* (exhibition catalogue).
        Baltimore: The Baltimore Museum of Art, 1982.

Serota, Nicholas, ed. *Bruce Nauman* (exhibition catalogue). London:
        Whitechapel Art Gallery, 1986. Essays by Joan Simon
        and Jean-Christophe Amman.

Van Bruggen, Coosje. *Bruce Nauman*. New York: Rizzoli Books, 1988.

Dennis **Oppenheim**

Sculpture still has a tremendous ability to surprise. Given that potential, we shouldn't be saddled with uninspired monoliths over and over again. Sculpture could still be extremely radical as a way station between architecture and the environment. I am attempting to tap that potential by considering structure— the way the pieces look—to be subservient to something greater; I'm trying to get art to operate in a temperate zone that exists between mind and matter.

Quoted in Ellen Schwartz, "Dennis Oppenheim: Art Between Mind and Matter," *ArtNews*, 81 (December 1982), pp. 55-56.

Lecture #1, 1976–83

Wood and aluminum mannequin with felt suit, steel lectern
with brass lamp, 48 wood chairs, and stereo recording: mannequin,
29 1/2 x 13 x 13 inches; lectern, 23 1/2 x 15 x 21 inches; chairs,
17 1/2 x 7 3/4 x 7 3/4 inches each
Whitney Museum of American Art, New York;
Gift of Professor Donald Wall   83.38a-xx

Lecture #1
Dennis Oppenheim

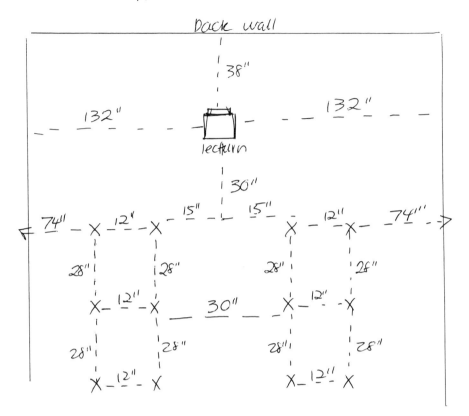

Chairs (48 total) positioned in four rows of
twelve as diagramed above. Lectern light
should be on at all times. Figure's hands
should rest on lectern including the arm
up to the elbow. Electrical parts (tape
recorder, etc.) should be hidden as much
as possible. Room should be a neutral
color, such as gray. Lighting could
be low or medium. general lighting
for the room itself - an elepsodial spotlight
should be hung from the ceiling and
directed in the area of the figure &
the lectern.
Speakers should be wall mounted,
near the ceiling

tape recording should be repeated twice
every hour on the hour

Audiotape **Transcript**

I would like to welcome you here tonight. Many years have passed since we have seen each other. Some of you may know, my eyesight has grown progressively worse, and although I cannot see you, I feel your presence. I will begin tonight's lecture by refreshing your memory regarding some basic art historical facts; facts that you now realize are the basis for the conspiracy that continues to plague us. Let us begin with the summer of 1973 in Amarillo, Texas, with the death of Robert Smithson, the American sculptor. In recalling that period most of us had no reason to believe the circumstances were anything but accidental. The aircraft simply lost control; the motor failed, he died. There were no suspicions. Four years later on July 12, 1977, sixty miles south of Las Vegas, Nevada, Walter De Maria committed suicide. He was preparing the final details concerning the installation of his lightening rod project in the desert. The art community was shocked but the investigation uncovered no circumstances that could be considered abnormal. I became suspicious. On September 11, 1977, four years after Robert Smithson's death, Michael Helzer, the American earth artist, was found trampled to death outside his trailer east of Reno, Nevada. As far as I was concerned, my suspicions were justified. All three of these artists worked within a similar sensibility, that of large, land based projects. The coincidence was overwhelming. The art community became slightly edgy. This discomfort broke into mild hysteria when on January 15, 1979, a Boeing 747 en route to Copenhagen exploded off the coast of Sweden; all the passengers were killed. On board were Carl Andre, Robert Morris, Bruce Nauman, Lawrence Weiner, Joseph Kosuth, Robert Barry, and William Wegman. Bomb fragments were discovered within the wreckage and the reports termed the situation "bizarre." Apparently, the placement of the bomb in proximity of the passengers created rather unusual after-effects. It was now overwhelmingly obvious that we were in the midst of a conspiracy. American artists whom had surfaced during the sixties were the target of a carefully planned series of assassinations beginning in 1973 with the death of Robert Smithson. I have always believed this, although with Smithson's death I had no direct clues. Meanwhile, I began preparing myself for what I felt would be the slow and complete annihilation of the American avant garde. A methodical masterplan, spread over perhaps twenty years, but successfully wiping out the backbone of American art. My first performance project using a marionette as a stand-in was tested in 1973. Many felt this was just another extension of myself, similar to the performance projects in which I involved my children in activities which spread or passed on my actions. However, behind the early performance figures was a mounting paranoia that shortly, if I remained surfaced, I too would become a victim of assassination. I was not able to detect any theme or consistent patterns in the deaths of the early victims, Smithson, De Maria, Helzer, outside of the obvious relationship of their work. I did, however, after the plane crash over Sweden in 1979 notice underlying abstract connections that are often found in the methodology or logic used in artmaking. On September 19, 1980, eight months after the crash of the Boeing 747, Vito Acconci fell down an open elevator shaft of his mother's apartment building in the South Bronx. Because of my close relationship with Acconci, I was notified immediately of this tragedy and did, in fact, rush to the Bronx. It was then that I knew my suspicions were warranted. There was an artist behind these acts. The individual acts were facets within an evolving larger work. Acconci's body lie in the basement of the tenement building. He had dropped fourteen floors. There were spears of intersecting light patterns jabbing into his body from the cracks in the basement ceiling. They produced an almost perfect grid over the body, containing it in six squares. God knows how a body lands after a fall, a fall almost two hundred feet. But I have never seen a position like this; he was completely rigid. His right side pressed into the soft earth of the shaft's floor, showing only the left side...he looked more as if he had risen from the ground than fallen from a great distance. His body was magically integrated within the space. As the authorities pulled Acconci from this tomb of intersecting light patterns, the imprint of his body appeared. It seemed more related to art than to death. For the next few months I emersed myself in the examination of facts and details pertaining to what now amounted to the death of eleven artists all of which occurred between 1973-1980. I was not alone in my interrogation of these actions. I remember only too clearly back in 1970, twenty-five years ago, speculating on the art of the 80's feeling out the sensations of my own development, testing hypothetically the duration of particular sensibilities in terms of change. The 80's always appeared dark and mysterious somehow. The rhythm in my own work did not make the sufficient leap to afford a perspective into the future. When the eighties came upon us with Acconci's death the new art suddenly showed itself. In some way our individual objective gave way to a union of investigation, our work became an instrument to combat what seemed to be happening to us. The 80s bred "the art of survival". Artists became investigators. The purpose of the American avant garde was to break the code, trace the connections, feel out the rhythms, and shed light on what seemed to be an untranslatable aesthetic masterplan set into motion by presumably an artist. As victims continued to fall during the winter of 1981 (Robert Ryman and Keith Sonnier were taken within the same week) the better galleries began to close. Their attempts to absorb new artists to replace the growing number of assassination victims failed. Mediocrity prevailed in most of the Art community. Critical writing focused on the more lightweight developments for fear of implication or association with the aesthetics of possible victims of assassination. My new projects continued with surrogate performances. The inclusion of an Audio System built into the figures started in the mid-seventies. This device allowed me to inject live voices into the figures from offstage. These indirect performances became less frequent because the risk of even being in close proximity to the work was too great. All the strong dance companies of the late sixties were wiped out...Yvonne Rainer, Joan Jonas, and Trisha Brown died during their performances. Musicians such as Phil Glass and Steve Reich went into hiding but reports suggested that Glass had been the victim of a head-on collision in the south of France. There had been no news of Steve Reich in fifteen years. Of course, I too, went into hiding. The South Houston area of New York became a barren landscape of foreclosed buildings. Some commercial industries moved into the area and in an attempt to save it from complete deterioration but generally it was known as New York's ghost town, like a stage set, it was no longer real. Landlords defaulted. Squatters began to occupy most of the buildings on West Broadway such as 420, which became the home of heroin addicts. Only two galleries remained in that area throughout this period, but, needless to say, the caliber of work they exhibited bordered on department store art and its proprietors had no way of relating to any sense of recent art history. Meetings of artists which proliferated during the 70s in an attempt to confront this wave of what became known as "aesthetics of assassination" came to a halt when an entire room full of panelists and the audience were machine gunned Chicago-style, leaving only three members of the underground alive. Even that seemingly classical method of execution had the constituents of a performance or some considered art activity. One survivor spoke of bursts of machine gun fire projected from four corners. The type of cartridge used was a tracer shell which produces traces of the trajectory, causing, during the peak volley, a perfect dissection of the room from corner to corner. On November 16, 1987, an attempt was made on my life. It was only due to bizarre circumstances that I escaped only wounded. This was not uncommon. Several artists escaped assassination during this period. Never at any point were there any clues left leading to suspects. Somehow, even though the grand scale and exactness of these acts suggested an army or at least a well organized group, the inside feeling, that is, the feeling of the remaining victims, were that these acts were produced by one person.

Born in Mason City (now Electric City), Washington, 1938
Studied at the California College of Arts and Crafts, Oakland (B.F.A., 1963); Stanford University, Palo Alto (M.F.A., 1965)
Lives in New York

SELECTED ONE-ARTIST EXHIBITIONS

1968   John Gibson Gallery, New York
1969   Galerie Yvon Lambert, Paris
        Galerie Françoise Lambert, Milan
1970   John Gibson Gallery, New York
1971   Galerie Yvon Lambert, Paris
1972   Sonnabend Gallery, New York
        Tate Gallery, London
1973   Galerie Sonnabend, Paris
        Mayor Gallery, London
1974   Stedelijk Museum, Amsterdam
        John Gibson Gallery, New York
1975   The Kitchen, New York
1976   M.L. d'Arc Gallery, New York
1977   Fine Arts Gallery at Wright State University, Dayton, Ohio
1978   Visual Arts Gallery, School of Visual Arts, New York
1979   Kunsthalle Basel, Switzerland
1980   Portland Center for the Visual Arts, Oregon
1981   Contemporary Arts Center, Cincinnati
1983   Munson-Williams-Proctor Institute Musuem of Art, Utica, New York
        Whitney Museum of American Art, New York
1984   Braunstein Gallery, San Francisco
        San Francisco Museum of Modern Art
        La Jolla Museum of Contemporary Art, California

SELECTED GROUP EXHIBITIONS

1968   Dwan Gallery, New York, "Earthworks"
        Whitney Museum of American Art, New York, "1968 Annual Exhibition: Contemporary American Sculpture"

1969   Museum of Modern Art, New York, "New Media—New Methods"
1970   Museum of Modern Art, New York, "Information"
1971   Whitney Museum of American Art, New York, "1971 Annual Exhibition: Contemporary American Sculpture"
1974   The Clocktower, Institute for Art and Urban Resources, New York, "Words and Works"
1975   The Clocktower, Institute for Art and Urban Resources, New York "Selections from the Vogel Collection"
1976   Venice, Italy, "37th Biennale di Venezia"
1977   Kassel, West Germany, "Documenta 6"
        The New Museum, New York, "Early Works by Five Contemporary Artists"
        Whitney Museum of American Art, New York, "1977 Biennial Exhibition"
1979   The Detroit Institute of Arts, "Object and Image in Contemporary Sculpture"
        Museum of Contemporary Art, Chicago, "Concept, Narrative, Document"
1981   Whitney Museum of American Art, New York, "1981 Biennial"
        Hirshhorn Museum and Sculpture Garden, Smithsonian Institution, Washington, D.C., "Metaphor"
        Neuberger Museum, State University of New York at Purchase, "Soundings"
1984   University Art Museum, The University of New Mexico, Albuquerque, "Bruce Nauman/Dennis Oppenheim: Drawings and Models for Albuquerque Commissions"

SELECTED BIBLIOGRAPHY

Baker, Kenneth. "Dennis Oppenheim." *Arts Magazine*, 8 (April 1975), pp. 72-74.
Felshin, Nina. "Constructions II: Dennis Oppenheim." *Dialogue*, 3 (March-April 1981), pp. 19-21.
Sharp, Willoughby. "Interview with Dennis Oppenheim." *Studio International*, no. 182 (November 1971), pp. 186-193.

Judy **Pfaff**

*I am interested in opening up the language of sculpture
as far and as wide as I can in terms of materials, colors, and
references, and in trying to include all the things that are
permissible in painting but absent in sculpture. By attempting
to achieve a certain type of speed that is traditionally reserved
for painters, I'm reaching for a crossing over of ideas and a
weaving of thinking and making....Most parts of my work
are controlled and muscled into place, but there also exists
a natural, beautiful line. It is important that the work has a
balance of enough artifice and enough casualness, and
enough surprise and enough reason.*

Quoted in Richard Marshall and Robert Mapplethorpe, *Fifty New York Artists*
(San Francisco: Chronicle Books, 1986), p. 90.

Supermercado, 1986

Painted wood and metal, twenty-five units, 100 1/2 x 163 3/4 x 50 inches overall

Whitney Museum of American Art, New York; Purchase, with funds from the

Louis and Bessie Adler Foundation, Inc., Seymour M. Klein, President, and the

Sondra and Charles Gilman, Jr. Foundation, Inc.   86.34a-y

Deepwater, 1980

Installation at Holly Solomon Gallery, New York, 1980.

Dragon, 1981

Installation in "1981 Biennial Exhibition,"

Whitney Museum of American Art, New York, 1981.

N.Y.C. — B.Q.E., 1987

Installation in "1987 Biennial Exhibition,"

Whitney Museum of American Art, New York, 1987.

Born in London, 1946

Studied at Wayne State University, Detroit (1965–66); Southern Illinois University, Edwardsville (1968-69); Washington University, St. Louis (B.F.A., 1971); Yale University Summer School of Music and Art, Norfolk, Connecticut (1970); Yale University, New Haven (M.F.A., 1973)

Lives in New York

SELECTED ONE-ARTIST EXHIBITIONS

1974   Webb and Parsons Gallery, Bedford, New York
1975   Artists Space, New York
1980   Holly Solomon Gallery, New York
1981   John and Mable Ringling Museum of Art, Sarasota, Florida
1982   Albright-Knox Art Gallery, Buffalo
        The Bennington Museum, Bennington College, Vermont
        University Gallery, University of Massachusetts, Amherst
1985   Wacoal Art Center, Tokyo
1986   Knight Gallery-Spirit Square Center for the Arts, Charlotte, North Carolina
        Holly Solomon Gallery, New York

SELECTED GROUP EXHIBITIONS

1975   Whitney Museum of American Art, New York, "1975 Biennial Exhibition"
1979   Neuberger Museum, State University of New York at Purchase, "Ten Artists/Artists Space"
1980   Contemporary Arts Museum, Houston, "Extensions: Jennifer Bartlett, Lynda Benglis, Robert Longo, Judy Pfaff"
1981   Whitney Museum of American Art, New York, "1981 Biennial Exhibition"
        Hirshhorn Museum and Sculpture Garden, Smithsonian Institution, Washington, D.C., "Directions 1981"

Hayden Gallery, Massachusetts Institute of Technology, Cambridge, "Body Language: Figurative Aspects of Recent Art"
1983   Rheinisches Landesmuseum Bonn, "Back to the USA: Amerikanische Kunst der Siebziger und Achtziger" (traveled)
        Tate Gallery, London, "New Art"
1984   The Museum of Modern Art, New York, "An International Survey of Recent Painting and Sculpture"
        Venice, Italy, "41st Biennale di Venezia"
1985   The Brooklyn Museum, New York, "Working in Brooklyn: Sculpture"
        University Gallery, University of Massachusetts, Amherst, "Ten"
        Wacoal Art Center, Tokyo, "Vernacular Abstractions"
1986   Whitney Museum of American Art, New York, "Recent Acquisitions"
        Museum of Fine Arts, Boston, "Boston Collects: Contemporary Painting and Sculpture"
1987   Whitney Museum of American Art, New York, "1987 Biennial Exhibition"

SELECTED BIBLIOGRAPHY

Armstrong, Richard. "Judy Pfaff." *Los Angeles Institute of Contemporary Art Journal*, 19 (June-July 1987), p. 33.

Auping, Michael. *Judy Pfaff: Installations, Collages and Drawings* (exhibition catalogue). Sarasota, Florida: John and Mable Ringling Museum of Art, 1981.

Krane, Susan, and William Currie. *Judy Pfaff* (exhibition catalogue). Buffalo, New York: Albright-Knox Art Gallery and Hallwalls, 1982.

Saunders, Wade. "Talking Objects: Interviews with Ten Younger Sculptors." *Art in America*, 73 (November 1985), pp. 130-31.

Smith, Roberta. *Judy Pfaff: Stone, Scissor, Paper* (exhibition catalogue). Tokyo: Wacoal Art Center, 1985.

Alan **Saret**

The state of mind of being in many parts of a network at once—of being a network! Simultaneous variety through the network. It's a reaching in all directions exactly....Describe all the relationships in the cosmos you are dreaming about. Include the various consciousnesses, suns, planets, animals and plants. Determine the physics which provide them and the philosophies which guide them in the forms their activities take.

Quoted in Klaus Kertess, *Alan Saret: Matter Into Aether*, exhibition catalogue (Newport Beach, California: Newport Harbor Art Museum, 1982), pp. 81-98.

True Jungle: Canopy Forest, 1968

Painted wire, 108 x 216 x 48 inches (variable)

Whitney Museum of American Art, New York; Purchase,

with funds from the Howard and Jean Lipman Foundation, Inc. 69.7

Installation **Instructions**

On a length of wall approximately 18 to 25 feet long, large nails are driven into the wall at ten to twelve prescribed locations. Individual wire sections are hung on the nails and another layer of wire sections are then hung onto the previous layer. A loose and active placement of layers of wire pieces gradually covers the wall and builds to a depth of approximately 4 feet in some areas. While the final form is partially predetermined by the nature of the material and the shapes of the individual pieces, the overall configuration will vary each time the piece is installed.

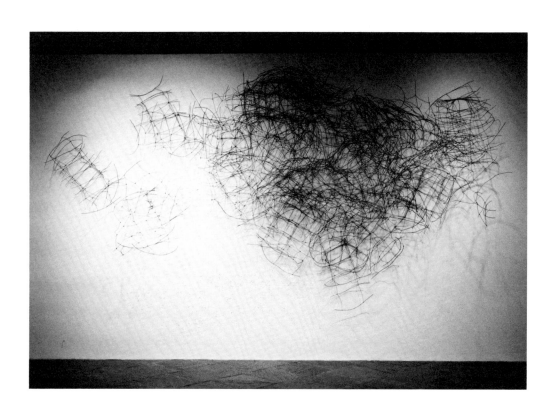

True Jungle: Canopy Forest, 1968

Installation in "Developments in Recent Sculpture,"

Whitney Museum of American Art, New York, 1981.

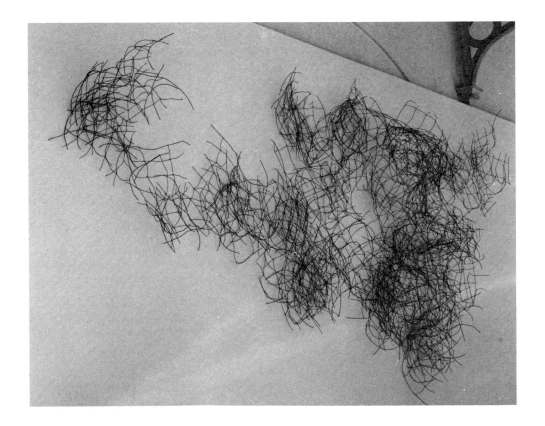

True Jungle: Canopy Forest, 1968

Installation in "Between Geometry and Gesture:

American Sculpture 1965-1975,"

Palacio de Velázquez, Madrid, 1986.

Born in New York, 1944
Studied at Cornell University, Ithaca, New York (B.A., 1966)
Lives in Brooklyn, New York

SELECTED ONE-ARTIST EXHIBITIONS

1968   Bykert Gallery, New York
1974   The Clocktower, Institute for Art and Urban Resources, New York
1977   Seattle Art Museum
1978   Fine Art Gallery, University of California, Irvine
1979   University Art Museum, University of California, Berkeley
       Hayden Gallery, Massachusetts Institute of Technology, Cambridge
1980   Charles Cowles Gallery, New York
1981   Galerie Rudolf Zwirner, Cologne
1982   Nigel Greenwood Gallery, London
       Newport Harbor Art Museum, Newport Beach, California
1983   Daniel Weinberg Gallery, Los Angeles
       Albright-Knox Art Gallery, Buffalo
1986   Margo Leavin Gallery, Los Angeles
1987   Christine Burgin Gallery, New York

SELECTED GROUP EXHIBITIONS

1968   Allen Memorial Art Museum, Oberlin College, Ohio, "Three Young Americans"
1969   Leo Castelli Gallery, New York, "Nine in a Warehouse"
1975   Artpark, Lewiston, New York, "The Ghosthouse"
1977   Museum of Contemporary Art, Chicago, "View of a Decade"
1979   The Museum of Modern Art, New York, "Contemporary Sculpture: Selections from the Collection of the Museum of Modern Art"
1981   Whitney Museum of American Art, New York, "Developments in Recent Sculpture"

1985   The Brooklyn Museum, New York, "Working in Brooklyn: Sculpture"
1986   Hayden Gallery, Massachusetts Institute of Technology, Cambridge, "Natural Forms and Forces"
       Palacio de Velázquez, Madrid, "Between Geometry and Gesture: American Sculpture 1965–1975"
1987   Whitney Museum of American Art, New York, "1987 Biennial Exhibition"

SELECTED BIBLIOGRAPHY

Armstrong, Richard, and Richard Marshall, eds. *Between Geometry and Gesture: American Sculpture 1965–1975* (exhibition catalogue). Madrid: Palacio de Velázquez, 1986.

Baker, Kenneth. "Alan Saret at the Albright-Knox and Hallwalls." *Art in America*, 71 (May 1983), p. 177.

Crary, Jonathan. "Alan Saret." *Arts Magazine*, 52 (September 1977), p. 4.

Kertess, Klaus. *Alan Saret: Matter into Aether* (exhibition catalogue). Newport Beach, California: Newport Harbor Art Museum, 1982.

Marshall, Richard. *Developments in Recent Sculpture* (exhibition catalogue). New York: Whitney Museum of American Art, 1981.

Wasserman, Emily. "Alan Saret, Bykert Gallery." *Artform*, 7 (January 1969), p. 59.

Richard **Serra**

Drawing is a concentration on an essential activity and the credibility of the statement is totally within your hands. It's the most direct, conscious space in which I work. I can observe my process from beginning to end, and at times sustain a continuous concentration. It's replenishing. It's one of the few conditions in which I can understand the source of my work....I think blackness is a property, not a quality.... the weight of the drawing doesn't derive from the number of layers of paintstick but from the shape of the drawing. A square, for example, carries more weight as a mass than does a rectangle....Shapes themselves refer to their internal masses....I no longer wanted to make markings on a piece of paper: I wanted to make the drawing integral to its structure and properties. What I continually find to be true is that the concentration I apply to drawing is a way of tuning or honing my eye. The more I draw, the better I see and the more I understand. There's always been a correlation between the strength of the work and the degree to which I'm drawing.

Quoted in Richard Serra and Lizzie Borden, "About Drawing," in *Richard Serra: Interviews, Etc. 1970-1980*, ed. Clara Weyergraf (Yonkers, New York: The Hudson River Museum, 1980), pp. 76-91.

Left Corner Rectangles, 1979

Oil paintstick on linen, two parts, 147 x 107 inches each

Whitney Museum of American Art, New York; 50th Anniversary Gift of the Louis

and Bessie Adler Foundation, Inc., Seymour M. Klein, President, and the Gilman

Foundation, Inc.   80.2

Installation **Instructions**

The left corner of the wall must be made a perfectly plumb right angle before the work is installed. Depending on how the work has been stored and rolled you will be able to determine placement, which means whether you will unroll the canvas starting from the right or from the left side. The canvasses have to be completely flush into the corner and must touch each other from top to bottom. The canvasses must be pulled tight and must be stapled firmly around their perimeters.

Untitled, 1979
Oil paintstick on linen, three parts, 108 x 258 x 180 inches overall
Installation in "1979 Biennial Exhibition," Whitney Museum of American Art,
New York, 1979.

Egyptian Horse Mix Squared to the Floor, 1979

Oil paintstick on linen, 130 x 156 inches

Leo Castelli Gallery, New York

Born in San Francisco, 1939
Studied at the University of California, Santa Barbara (B.A., 1961);
Yale University, New Haven (M.F.A., 1964)
Lives in New York

SELECTED ONE-ARTIST EXHIBITIONS

1968	Galerie Ricke, Cologne
1969	Leo Castelli Gallery, New York
1970	Ace Gallery, Los Angeles
	Pasadena Art Museum, California
1974	Leo Castelli Gallery, New York
	Visual Arts Gallery, School of Visual Arts, New York
1977	Stedelijk Museum, Amsterdam (traveled)
1978	Blum Helman Gallery, New York
	Museum of Modern Art, Oxford, England
1979	University Art Museum, University of California, Berkeley
1980	The Hudson River Museum, Yonkers, New York
	Museum Boymans-van Beuningen, Rotterdam
1981	Blum Helman Gallery, New York
	Leo Castelli Gallery, New York
1983	Musée National d'Art Moderne, Centre Georges Pompidou, Paris
1984	Leo Castelli Gallery, New York
1985	Museum Haus Lange, Krefeld, West Germany
1986	The Museum of Modern Art, New York

SELECTED GROUP EXHIBITIONS

1968	Whitney Museum of American Art, New York, "1968 Annual Exhibition: Contemporary American Sculpture"
1969	Kunsthalle Bern, Switzerland, "Live in Your Head: When Attitudes Become Form (Works—Concepts—Processes—Situations—Information) (traveled)
1970	Galleria d'Arte Moderna, Turin, Italy, "Conceptual Art/Art Povera/Land Art"
	The Museum of Modern Art, New York, "Information"

	Whitney Museum of American Art, New York, "1970 Annual Exhibition: Contemporary American Sculpture"
1971	Los Angeles County Museum of Art, "Art and Technology"
	Walker Art Center, Minneapolis, "Works for New Spaces"
1972	Kassel, West Germany, "Documenta 5"
1973	Whitney Museum of American Art, New York, "1973 Biennial Exhibition
1976	The Museum of Modern Art, New York, "Drawing Now" (traveled)
1977	Kassel, West Germany, "Documenta 6"
	Whitney Museum of American Art, New York, "1977 Biennial Exhibition"
1980	Hayden Gallery, Massachusetts Institute of Technology, Cambridge, "Mel Bochner/Richard Serra"
1981	Whitney Museum of American Art, New York, "1981 Biennial Exhibition"
1982	Kassel, West Germany, "Documenta 7"
	The Solomon R. Guggenheim Museum, New York, "New York School: Four Generations"
1985	Renaissance Society at the University of Chicago, "Large Scale Drawings by Sculptors"
	Museum of Art, Carnegie Institute, Pittsburgh, "1985 Carnegie International"
1986	Palacio de Velázquez, Madrid, "Between Geometry and Gesture: American Sculpture 1965–1975"

SELECTED BIBLIOGRAPHY

Halbreich, Kathy. *Mel Bochner/Richard Serra* (exhibition catalogue). Cambridge, Massachusetts: Hayden Gallery, Massachusetts Institute of Technology, 1980.

Krauss, Rosalind E. *Passages in Modern Sculpture.* New York: The Viking Press, 1977.

_____. *Richard Serra, Sculpture* (exhibition catalogue). New York: The Museum of Modern Art, 1986.

Weyergraf, Clara, ed. *Richard Serra: Interviews, Etc. 1970–1980* (exhibition catalogue). Yonkers, New York: The Hudson River Museum, 1980.

George **Sugarman**

An artist's reality is absolute. Even if uncertainty is his theme, the artist's version of it is, at any moment, unqualified. There is no conflict between these positions. With every step you take around a piece of sculpture, a new relationship is revealed. Reality, likewise, has no sides.

My own work is made up of these varying relationships, as one form is placed adjacent to another, sometimes absurdly, sometimes more logically. But each piece structures the space it moves through and implies the space it might continue to move through, giving the spectator a clue to a more ultimate relationship than that implied between each of the individual forms.

Quoted in Irving Sandler, *Recent American Sculpture*, exhibition catalogue (New York: The Jewish Museum, 1964), p. 9.

Inscape, 1964

Painted wood, 28 x 158 x 115 inches (variable)

Whitney Museum of American Art, New York; Purchase,

with funds from the Painting and Sculpture Committee   86.10a-i

Installation **Instructions**

Inscape forms a loop, more rectangular than round, but irregular. There is some freedom in putting it together but not much, though if I were creating it today I might make it much more loose.

But this is how it goes: First place the green form on the ground with the narrowest short end inward. The white form goes around it, with the gray form to your right as you are facing inwards. (All directions assume you are at the closed end of the white).

The long orange form with the open box comes next. Place it alongside the left side of the white, starting about a foot down and about fifteen inches to the side of the white, at a small angle to the left. The orange forms then goes, at an almost 90 degree angle to the left, then turns forward and then to the right again with the long narrow form.

The large 3-colored form (red, black and off-white) is the heaviest and must be placed with care so that the red arm comes over the first extension of the orange while the last mentioned orange form goes under the black and comes out alongside the off-white. The orange forms then meet again, a small gap between them, with the roughly semi-circular forms placed so that its other part, the repetitive open forms, crosses over the off-white where it meets the twisting linear open form that goes outward. Its end is met by the block-like forms that touch it and go inward toward the green. The irregular cross form goes over the open diamond, stretching toward but not quite going over the green.

Inscape, 1964

Inscape II, 1985

Painted aluminum, 48 x 180 x 216 inches (variable)

Collection of the artist

Born in the Bronx, New York, 1912
Studied at City College of New York (B.A., 1938);
Zadkine School of Sculpture, Paris (1955-56)
Lives in New York

SELECTED ONE-ARTIST EXHIBITIONS

1960	Widdifield Gallery, New York
1961	Stephen Radich Gallery, New York
1967	Fischbach Gallery, New York
	Galerie Renée Ziegler, Zurich
	Galerie Alfred Schmela, Düsseldorf
1969	Kunsthalle Basel, Switzerland
1974	Zabriskie Gallery, New York
1977	Robert Miller Gallery, New York
1980	Robert Miller Gallery, New York
	Galerie Rudolf Zwirner, Cologne
1981	Joslyn Art Museum, Omaha, Nebraska
	Galerie Renée Ziegler, Zurich
	Museum of Fine Arts, Springfield, Massachusetts
1982	Robert Miller Gallery, New York
1984	Fuller Goldeen Gallery, San Francisco
1985	Whitney Museum of American Art, New York

SELECTED GROUP EXHIBITIONS

1952	Musée Rodin, Paris, "IVe Salon de la Jeune Sculpture"
1958	Hansa Gallery, New York, "New Sculpture Show"
1959	Stable Gallery, New York, "New Sculpture Group"
1963	The Art Institute of Chicago, "65th American Exhibition"
	Wadsworth Atheneum, Hartford, "Continuity and Change: 45 American Abstract Painters and Sculptors"
	São Paulo, Brazil, "VII Bienal de São Paulo" (traveled)
1964	The Jewish Museum, New York, "Recent American Sculpture"
1967	Los Angeles County Museum of Art, "American Sculpture of the Sixties" (traveled)
1968	Whitney Museum of American Art, New York, "1968 Annual Exhibition: Contemporary American Sculpture"
1975	Portland Art Museum, Oregon, "Masterworks in Wood: The Twentieth Century"
	National Collection of Fine Arts, Smithsonian Institution, Washington, D.C., "Sculpture: American Directions 1945-1975" (traveled)
1976	Whitney Museum of American Art, "200 Years of American Sculpture"
1979	Institute of Contemporary Art, University of Pennsylvania, Philadelphia, "The Decorative Impulse" (traveled)
1982	Contemporary Arts Museum, Houston, "The Americans: The Collage"
1984	Whitney Museum of American Art, New York, "The Third Dimension: Sculpture of the New York School" (traveled)
1985	The Museum of Modern Art, New York, "Contemporary Works from the Collection"

SELECTED BIBLIOGRAPHY

Althus, Peter F., Amy Goldin, and Irving H. Sandler. *George Sugarman: Plastiken, Collagen, Zeichnungen* (exhibition catalogue). Basel, Switzerland: Kunsthalle Basel, 1969.

Day, Holliday T., and Brad Davis. *Shapes of Space: The Sculpture of George Sugarman* (exhibition catalogue). Omaha, Nebraska: Joslyn Art Museum, 1981.

Phillips, Lisa. *George Sugarman: Painted Wood Sculpture* (exhibition catalogue). New York: Whitney Museum of American Art, 1985.

_____. *The Third Dimension: Sculpture of the New York School* (exhibition catalogue). New York: Whitney Museum of American Art, 1984.

Sandler, Irving H. *American Sculpture of the Sixties* (exhibition catalogue). Los Angeles: Los Angeles County Museum of Art, 1967.

James **Turrell**

The first image was essentially a rectangle projected across a corner in such a way that from a distance there appeared to be a cube floating off the floor, yet in some manner attached to the corner of the space. From a distance this shape had solidity, but appeared to be literally composed of light. Still at a distance, but moving to the side, one could further substantiate this impression because the cube seemed to reveal itself in perspective. Advancing toward the image, the image would eventually dissolve to the point where you saw not the object in space, but the actual light on the wall.

The first images all had a distinctive sculptural quality: the piece seemed to objectify and make physically present light as a tangible material. The space which these pieces occupied was definitely not the same as that which the room had without the image. The space generated was analogous to a painting in two dimensions alluding to three dimensions, but in this case three-dimensional space was being used illusionistically. That is, the forms engendered through this quality of illusion did not necessarily resolve into one clearly definable form that would exist in three dimensions....Throughout the series, the image had a sense of solidity because in some manner a quality of transparency and surface had been created. To some degree the feeling of transparency and surface was unavoidable since the image was formed across a corner actually existing in three dimensions, and because any evenly lit shape of light projected on the wall cannot ride on exactly the same plane as the wall.

Quoted in Barbara Haskell, *James Turrell: Light and Space*, exhibition catalogue (New York: Whitney Museum of America Art, 1981), p. 15.

Afrum, 1967

Xenon light projection, dimensions variable

Collection of Giuseppe Panza di Biumo

Installation **Instructions**

Projector mounted from ceiling; room must be at least 24 by 24 feet...ceiling height must be between 11 to 14 feet.

The two walls (at right angles) must be prepared with a plaster or joint-compound slip coat that extends from the corner at least 15 feet down each wall.

No other light in room space; no direct light into the area from another space...at least near the image; no grates or air conditioning ducts in the near vicinity.

Center of image is 62 inches above floor.

The subject is your seeing, the ideas are wordless, and it was executed in the second year after I became an artist.

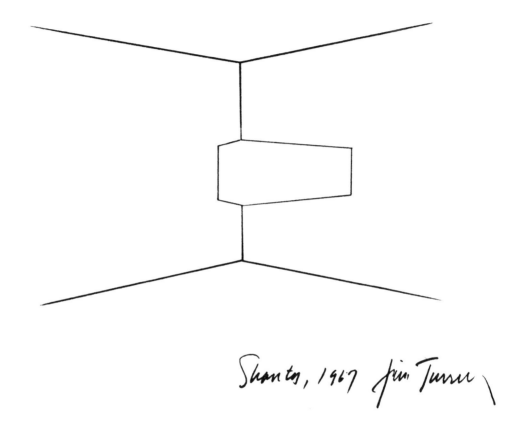

Shanta, 1967 Jim Turrell

Original drawing left at Pasadena Art Mus. Redrawn 1975

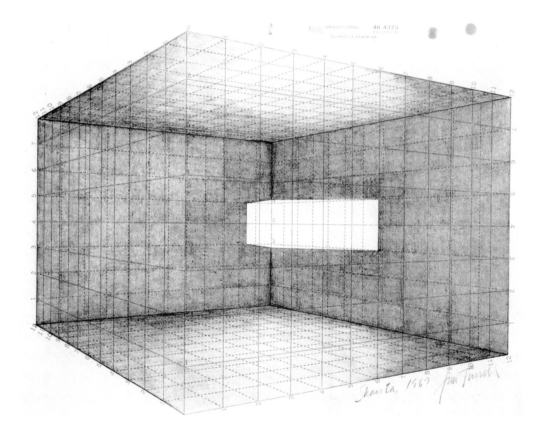

Study for *Shanta*, 1967

Graphite on paper, 17 x 19 1/2 inches

Private collection

Born in Los Angeles, 1943
Studied at Pomona College, Claremont, California (B.A., 1965);
University of California, Irvine (1965–66)
Lives in Flagstaff, Arizona.

SELECTED ONE-ARTIST EXHIBITIONS

1967   Pasadena Art Museum, California
1976   Stedelijk Museum, Amsterdam
       ARCO Center for Visual Art, Los Angeles
1980   University of Arizona Museum of Art, Tuscon
       Whitney Museum of American Art, New York
       Leo Castelli Gallery, New York
1981   Herron School of Art Gallery, Indiana University—
       Purdue University, Indianapolis
       Portland Center for the Visual Arts, Oregon
1982   Center on Contemporary Art, Seattle
       The Israel Museum, Jerusalem
1983   Hayden Gallery, Massachusetts Institute of Technology,
       Cambridge
       Flow Ace Gallery, Venice, California
       University Art Gallery, University of Delaware, Newark
       Musée d'Art Moderne de la Ville de Paris
1984   Flow Ace Gallery, Venice, California
       Capp Street Project, San Francisco
       Bernard Jacobson Gallery, Los Angeles
1985   Marian Goodman Gallery, New York
       The Museum of Contemporary Art, Los Angeles

SELECTED GROUP EXHIBITIONS

1968   Los Angeles County Museum of Art, "Art and Technology"
1975   La Jolla Museum of Contemporary Art, California,
       "University of California, Irvine, 1965–1975"
1981   Louisiana Museum, Humlebaek, Denmark, "Drawing
       Distinctions: American Drawings of the Seventies"
       (traveled)

1982   The Art Institute of Chicago, "74th American Exhibition"
1985   École des Beaux-Arts, Paris, "Menil Collection"
       San Francisco Museum of Modern Art, "Art &
       Architecture & Landscape: The Clos Pegase Design
       Competition"

SELECTED BILBIOGRAPHY

Adney, Carol. *Avaar, A Light Installation* (exhibition catalogue).
    Indianapolis: Herron School of Art Gallery, Indiana
    University—Purdue Uninversity, 1980.

Brown, Julia, ed. *Occluded Front: James Turrell* (exhibition
    catalogue). Los Angeles: The Museum of Contemporary
    Art, 1985.

Coplans, John. *Jim Turrell* (exhibition catalogue). Pasadena,
    California: Pasadena Art Museum, 1967.

de Wilde, Edy, ed. *James Turrell* (exhibition catalogue).
    Amsterdam: Stedelijk Museum, 1976.

Haskell, Barbara. *James Turrell: Light and Space* (exhibition
    catalogue). New York: Whitney Museum of American
    Art, 1980.

Wortz, Melinda. *University of California, Irvine, 1965–75*. (exhibition
    catalogue). La Jolla, California: La Jolla Museum of
    Contemporary Art, 1975.

Richard **Tuttle**

In life you can do two things. In art you can do one thing. There are no decisions to make in art except one — that is the possibility of art, while the actuality (of it) is life-like. And that is why anything connected with art appears paradoxical, although that is not the goal of art. Art is discipline and discipline is drawing. Drawing will change before art will. Discipline is always the same. And we will never know what art is — except as the goal, which already defined through necessity although not understood, is essentially abstract in nature or naturally abstracted, which is to say life-like, without hope. Because color is the more abstract evidence of/in art and because we are beginning to grasp certain specific abstracted experiences (which appear as forms in art) my work looks the way it does.

Richard Tuttle, "150 Words on My Work," *Art International*, 12 (May 15, 1968), p. 48.

Grey Extended Seven, 1967

Dyed canvas, 48 1/2 x 59 1/2 inches

Whitney Museum of American Art, New York; Purchase, with funds

from the Simon Foundation, Inc. and the National Endowment for the Arts 75.7

Installation **Instructions**

Use brads for the cloth piece (push pins are too visually interesting). Use as few as possible, leaving the bottom loose to let the evil spirits out.

Installation view, "Anti-Illusion: Procedures/Materials,"

Whitney Museum of American Art, New York, 1969.

Drift III, 1965

Painted wood, 24 1/4 x 52 3/4 x 1 1/4 inches

Whitney Museum of American Art, New York; Purchase,

with funds from Mr. and Mrs. William A. Marsteller and

the Painting and Sculpture Committee   83.18

Fountain, 1965

Painted wood, 1 x 40 x 39 inches

Whitney Museum of American Art, New York;

50th Anniversary Gift of Richard Brown Baker   79.76

Born in Rahway, New Jersey, 1941

Studied at Trinity College, Hartford, Connecticut (B.A., 1963)

Lives in New York

SELECTED ONE-ARTIST EXHIBITIONS

1965	Betty Parsons Gallery, New York
1968	Betty Parsons Gallery, New York
1969	Nicholas Wilder Gallery, Los Angeles
1972	The Museum of Modern Art, New York
1974	Nigel Greenwood Gallery, London
1975	Whitney Museum of American Art, New York (traveled)
1978	Young Hoffman Gallery, Chicago
1979	Stedelijk Museum, Amsterdam
1983	Blum Helman Gallery, New York
1984	Daniel Weinberg Gallery, Los Angeles
1985	Städtisches Museum Abteiberg Mönchengladbach, West Germany
	Institute of Contemporary Arts, London
1986	CAPC Musée d'Art Contemporain, Bordeaux, France
1987	Neue Galerie Am Landesmuseum Joanneum, Graz, Austria

SELECTED GROUP EXHIBITIONS

1969	Kunsthalle Bern, Switzerland, "Live in Your Head: When Attitudes Become Form (Works—Concepts—Processes—Situations—Information)" (traveled)
	Whitney Museum of American Art, New York, "Anti-Illusion: Procedures/Materials"
1974	The Art Museum, Princeton University, New Jersey, "Line as Language: Six Artists Draw"
1975	The Baltimore Museum of Art, "14 Artists"
1977	Museum of Contemporary Art, Chicago, "A View of a Decade"
1980	Hayward Gallery, London, "Pier & Ocean: Construction in the Art of the Seventies" (traveled)

1982	Blum Helman Gallery, New York, "Ryman/Tuttle/Twombly: New Work"
1985	Whitney Mueum of American Art, New York, "Drawing Acquisitions, 1981–1985"
	Museum Haus Lange, Krefeld, West Germany, "In Offener Form"
	Westfälischer Kunstverein, Münster, "Wasserfarbenblätter von Joseph Beuys, Nicola De Maria, Gerhard Richter, Richard Tuttle"
1986	Fine Art Gallery, University of Arkansas at Little Rock, "Drawings from the Collection of Dorothy and Herbert Vogel" (traveled)
	Palacio de Velázquez: Madrid, "Between Geometry and Gesture: American Sculpture 1965–1975"

SELECTED BIBLIOGRAPHY

Graevenitz, Gerhard von. *Pier & Ocean: Construction in the Art of the Seventies* (exhibition catalogue). London: Hayward Gallery, 1980.

Krauss, Rosalind E. *Line as Language: Six Artists Draw* (exhibition catalogue). Princeton, New Jersey: The Art Museum, Princeton University, 1974.

Pincus-Witten, Robert. "The Art of Richard Tuttle." *Artforum*, 8 (February 1985), pp. 62-67.

Tucker, Marcia. *Richard Tuttle* (exhibition catalogue). New York: Whitney Museum of American Art, 1975.

Tuttle, Richard. *Richard Tuttle: Paris* (exhibition catalogue). Calais, France: Musée de Calais, 1982

Works in the **Exhibition**

All works are from the Permanent Collection of the
Whitney Museum of American Art. Dimensions are in
inches; height precedes width precedes depth.

Vito Acconci (b. 1940)
False Center for L.A. (or The New York Address), 1978–79
Painted wood construction, speakers, amplifier,
quadrophonic tape deck, and mushroom lamp,
96 1/2 x 49 3/4 x 49 3/4
Purchase, with funds from the Gilman Paper Company
and the National Endowment for the Arts   79.32

Carl Andre (b. 1935)
Twenty-Ninth Copper Cardinal, 1975
Twenty-nine copper plates, 3/16 x 20 x 20 each,
3/16 x 20 x 580 overall
Purchase, with funds from the Gilman Foundation, Inc.
and the National Endowment for the Arts   75.55

Mel Bochner (b. 1940)
Ten to 10, 1972
Stones, 120 diameter
Purchase, with funds from the Gilman Foundation, Inc.
77.28

Jonathan Borofsky (b. 1942)
Running People at 2,616,216, 1979
Latex paint on wall, dimensions variable
Purchase, with funds from the Painting and Sculpture
Committee   84.43

Dan Flavin (b. 1933)
Untitled (for Robert, with fond regards), 1977
Pink, yellow, and red fluorescent lights,
96 x 96 across the corner
Purchase, with funds from the Louis and Bessie Adler
Foundation, Inc., Seymour M. Klein, President,
the Howard and Jean Lipman Foundation, Inc., by
exchange, and gift of Peter M. Brant, by exchange
78.57

Alternate:
Untitled, 1966
White fluorescent lights,
96 x 21 x 3 1/2
Gift of Howard and Jean Lipman   71.214

Robert Irwin (b. 1928)
No Title, 1966–67
Acrylic on aluminum with four electric lights,
48 diameter x 13 deep
Purchase, with funds from the Howard and Jean Lipman
Foundation, Inc.   68.42

Sol LeWitt (b. 1928)

Lines to Points on a Six Inch Grid. 1st wall: 24 lines from the center; 2nd wall: 12 lines from the midpoint of each of the sides; 3rd wall: 12 lines from each corner; 4th wall: 24 lines from the center, 12 lines from the midpoint of each of the sides, 12 lines from each corner, 1976

White crayon lines and black pencil grid on black walls, dimensions variable

Purchase, with funds from the Gilman Foundation, Inc. 78.1.1-4

Mary Lucier (b. 1944)

Ohio at Giverny, 1983

Video installation: two videotapes, color, sound, 18-1/2 minutes; seven monitors, progressing in size from left to right, 13 inches, 15 inches, 15 inches, 17 inches, 19 inches, 21 inches, 21 inches; and synchronous starter, 97 x 268 x 198 (variable)

Purchase, with funds from the Louis and Bessie Adler Foundation, Inc., Seymour M. Klein, President, and Mrs. Rudolph B. Schulhof   83.35a-j

Bruce Nauman (b. 1941)

Untitled, 1965-66

Latex on burlap, 20 x 65 x 40 (variable)

Gift of Mr. and Mrs. Peter M. Brant   76.43

Dennis Oppenheim (b. 1938)

Lecture #1, 1976–83

Wood and aluminum mannequin with felt suit, steel lectern with brass lamp, forty-eight wood chairs, and stereo recording: mannequin, 29 1/2 x 13 x 13; lectern, 23 1/2 x 15 x 21; chairs, 17 1/2 x 7 3/4 x 7 3/4 each

Gift of Professor Donald Wall   83.38a-xx

Judy Pfaff (b. 1946)

Supermercado, 1986

Painted wood and metal, twenty-five units, 100 1/2 x 163 3/4 x 50 overall

Purchase, with funds from the Louis and Besie Adler Foundation, Inc., Seymour M. Klein, President, and the Sondra and Charles Gilman, Jr. Foundation, Inc. 86.34a-y

Alan Saret (b. 1944)

True Jungle: Canopy Forest, 1968

Painted wire, 108 x 216 x 48 (variable)

Purchase, with funds from the Howard and Jean Lipman Foundation, Inc.   69.7

Richard Serra (b. 1939)

Left Corner Rectangles, 1979

Oil paintstick on linen,

two parts, 147 x 107 each

50th Anniversary Gift of the Louis and Bessie Adler

Foundation, Inc., Seymour M. Klein, President,

and the Gilman Foundation, Inc.   80.2

George Sugarman (b. 1912)

Inscape, 1964

Painted wood, 28 x 158 x 115 (variable)

Purchase, with funds from the Painting and Sculpture

Committee   86.10a-i

Alternate:

Inscape II, 1985

Painted aluminum, 48 x 180 x 216 (variable)

Collection of the artist

James Turrell (b. 1943)

Shanta, 1967

Xenon light projection,

dimensions variable

Gift of Philip Johnson   81.29

Richard Tuttle (b. 1941)

Grey Extended Seven, 1967

Dyed canvas, 48 1/2 x 59 1/2

Purchase, with funds from the Simon Foundation, Inc.

and the National Endowment for the Arts   75.7